POETS OF THE 'NINETIES

BY THE SAME AUTHOR

Music for Statues (verse), Routledge & Kegan Paul
The Freedom of Poetry (critical essays), Falcon Press
Dylan Thomas: A Literary Study, Spearman
John Betjeman: A Study, Spearman
Prose of the Century (Editor), Nelson

AUBREY BEARDSLEY

DEREK STANFORD

Poets of the 'Nineties

A BIOGRAPHICAL ANTHOLOGY

JOHN BAKER
5 ROYAL OPERA ARCADE
PALL MALL, SW1

First published 1965 by
John Baker Publishers Limited
5 Royal Opera Arcade
Pall Mall, London
SW1

Printed in Great Britain by
W. & J. Mackay & Co Ltd, Chatham, Kent

TO

JOHN BAYLISS

'WITH WHOM I LEARNED MY TRADE'

Contents

CONTENTS

CONTENTS

Illustrations

Acknowledgements

The Author and Publishers wish to thank the following copyright-owners, trustees, and publishers for permission to include their copyright material in this book: The Bodley Head Ltd for poems by Victor Plarr, *In the Dorian Mood;* William Heinemann Ltd for poems by Arthur Symons from *The Poems of Arthur Symons;* Mrs W. B. Yeats and Messrs Macmillan and Co. Ltd for poems from *The Collected Poems of W. B. Yeats* and for quotations from Yeats's critical works; the Dominican Council, the Trustee of the English Province of the Order of Preachers, for the poems by John Gray; the Society of Authors as the literary representatives of the Estate of the late Richard le Gallienne, for poems by Richard le Gallienne; Edward Colman Esq., for the Lord Douglas Literary Estate, for poems by Lord Alfred Douglas; Mr Rupert Hart-Davis and Rupert Hart-Davis Ltd for extracts from the letters of Oscar Wilde.

The Author wishes also to record his personal indebtedness to Mr Ian Fletcher, editor of *The Complete Poems of Lionel Johnson* (1953), the Introduction and Notes to which constitute a storehouse of 'Nineties information.

Preface

FROM my sixteenth year I have had a devotion to the poets of the 'nineties. In my earlier days their personalities assumed for me a sort of legendary dimension; and with Arthur Symons, one of their number, I was near to identifying myself. Perhaps it is because 1965 marks the centenary of this writer's birth that I have been led to occupy myself with some re-sorting of these old enthusiasms.

There does not exist in print today a single selection from the poets of the 'nineties. When all other schools and eras—from Romantic, Georgian, to Imaginst—are served by accessible compilations, it seems unfortunate that *fin-de-siècle* verse should be without its due anthology. Nor has the period fared much better in the past. Between 1900 and the present day, so far as I know, there has only been made one representative collection of its poetry: A. J. A. Symons' *An Anthology of 'Nineties Verse*, published by the Bodley Head in 1928. This work, which was not re-issued, although of interest, had certain limitations. Its editor, the one-time possessor of an extensive library of the 'nineties, looked upon its literature with more of a collector's than a critic's eye. His choice emphasised the 'period' note, and many of the poems selected by him are rather curios than perennials. He also felt himself free to include any piece by a 'ninety-ish' poet whether actually written in that decade or not.

The present anthology is conceived within narrower limits. Outside of the critical comment provided, I have not reproduced any pieces here which were not published for the first time, in magazine or book-form, in the 'nineties.

My choice of poets has been made on an even stricter principle. Besides the poets of the 'nineties who wrote in a distinctly 'ninety-ish' style, there were, of course, other poets composing some of their best work between 1890 and 1900: Rudyard Kipling, W. E. Henley, A. E. Housman, Alice Meynell, and Francis Thompson, as well as such late-Victorian figures as Swinburne, Meredith, and Hardy. All of these poets formed a style independent of 'the style of the 'nineties'. Their ideas and diction derived from other sources than the decadence, impressionism and aestheticism which marked the exclusively *fin-de-siècle* verse. These poets I have therefore not included since they may severally be spoken of, with equal correctness, as poets of the 'sixties, 'seventies, 'eighties, nineteen-hundreds, and nineteen-tens.

My own selection of 'nineties poetry has been made from the 'ninety-ish' poets of that decade. Ten of the eleven poets I have chosen were members of the Rhymers Club, the short-lived *cénacle* of poets whose two anthologies provided a stamping-ground for the formation of the *fin-de-siècle* style. The only non-Rhymer poets included here are Oscar Wilde and Lord Alfred Douglas—the high-priest of aestheticism and the high-priest's favoured and gifted acolyte—and Aubrey Beardsley, art editor successively of *The Yellow Book* and *The Savoy*. Although the greater part of Wilde's poetry belonged to an earlier vintage, by force of his eloquence, pose, and wit he remained the almost undisputed *arbiter elegantiarum* of the decade until his downfall in 1895. After that date it was certainly Beardsley who did most to keep the Black Peter of decadence still provocatively flying. In selecting the poems I have included a number of translations from the French, since Paris was the movement's true literary capital.

A word as to the simple make-up of this book. I have followed my general Introduction with a preliminary notice on each one of the poets, printed at the head of the selections from their verse. In these notices I have attempted to present the reader with a free mosaic of information and opinion, not considering them the place for anything like organised formal criticism. The process of analysis and comparison obviously calls for more extensive treatment than my limited space permits; but if this anthology proves successful I shall hope to accord these poets such fuller assessment elsewhere. At the same time I have practised no self-denying ordinance, and have accordingly indulged myself in making whatever critical interpretations offered themselves in informal fashion.

In conclusion, I should like to record my thanks to Mrs Margaret Holdsworth, who read and typed the manuscripts, for her careful corrections and revisions. My gratitude is also due to my friend John Clifford Bayliss who, since our school days, has encouraged me in my 'nineties studies with researches of his own and the gift of many books.

Hampstead,
September 1964.

Poets of the 'Nineties

I

THERE are two things to remark in the poets of the 'nineties: the distinction of their work and the tragedy of their lives. The first is a fact, a critical commonplace; the second, a mystery still, a problem.

Utterly unlike, in their fevered existence, those 'bards who died content on pleasant sward,/Leaving great verse unto a little clan',[1] the poets of the 'nineties did leave their own clear record: 'a few evasive . . . snatches of song'[2]—output of a 'delicate . . . discriminating taste'.[3] Mallarmé had spoken of the artists' need to 'purify the dialect of the tribe' and this was what the 'nineties poets effected. They took the heterogenous speech of Victorian poetry and sought to refine it. Yeats has commented that 'in the Victorian era the most famous poetry was often a passage in a poem of some length, perhaps of great length, a poem full of thoughts that might have been expressed in prose'.[4] It was this prose element in verse that these poets desired to eliminate.

To the leading Victorian figures 'a short lyric had seemed an accident, an interruption amid more serious

[1] 'Fragment of an Ode to Maia, written on May Day 1818': *The Poetical Works of John Keats* (1915)
[2] 'Ernest Dowson' (*Studies in Prose and Verse*) by Arthur Symons (1904)
[3] 'The Tragic Generation' (*The Trembling of the Veil*) (1922)
[4] 'Modern Poetry' (*Essays and Introductions*) (1961)

work'[1]—the poet's expression on the problems of the day, on social, religious, or political issues. To the poets of the 'nineties, the lyric became the paradigm of all poetry. Its short highly cultivated span of perfection seemed to measure all that was mixed or unpoetic. 'We tried', recalled Yeats, 'to write like the poets of the Greek Anthology, or like Cutullus, or like the Jacobean lyricists, men who wrote while poetry was still pure.'[2] Verlaine had spoken of Victor Hugo as 'a supreme poet, but a volcano of mud as well as of flame'.[3] The 'nineties poets wished to be all flame, happy to settle for a light-weight perfection. 'Their poems seemed to say', as Yeats remarked, 'you will remember us the longer because we are very small, very unambitious.'[4] 'Yet my friends', continued Yeats, 'were most ambitious men; they wished to express life at its intense moments, those moments that are brief because of their intensity, and at those moments alone.'[5]

II

WAS there, one wonders, any occult connection between the nature, the distinction of this work, and the tragedies which their authors enacted? Yeats, who lived and moved among these poets, asked the question, and commented on a paradox. 'Why should men', he inquired, 'who spoke their opinions in low voices, as though they feared to disturb the readers in some ancient library, and timidly as though they knew that all subjects had long since been explored, all questions long since decided in

[1] Ibid.
[2] 'Modern Poetry' (*Essays and Introductions*)
[3] 'The Tragic Generation' (*The Trembling of the Veil*)
[4] 'Modern Poetry' (*Essays and Introductions*)
[5] Ibid.

books whereon the dust settled—live lives of such disorder . . . ?'[1]

Certainly the casualty figures are impressive. 'I have known twelve men who killed themselves', Arthur Symons, veteran and doyen of the decade, reflected in later life. Symons, himself a prey to madness in middle years, had perhaps his heightened way of putting things; yet sober statistics all point in the same direction. Ernest Dowson, dead of consumption at thirty-two; Lionel Johnson, dying from a stroke, a confirmed dipsomaniac, at thirty-five; John Davidson, a suicide, at fifty-three; Oscar Wilde, disgraced and imprisoned at the height of his career, then dying after three years barren exile, aged forty-six; Aubrey Beardsley (poet as well as artist), consumptive and dying at twenty-six.

And these were only the front-rank figures. Other casualties, among the friends of these men, would include William Theodore Peters, actor and poet, who died of starvation in Paris; Hubert Crackanthorpe, short-storyist, who threw himself into the Seine; Francis Adams, novelist and essayist, who died by his own hand; Henry Harland, editor of *The Yellow Book*, who died of consumption at forty-three; Francis Thompson, kept alive on opium, who died of the same disease at forty-eight; Charles Conder, rococo fan-painter, who died in an asylum, aged forty-one.

To this asylum, in 1908, Arthur Symons was sent after the attack of madness which came upon him in Italy. From its effects he never fully recovered. Yeats, alone almost, lived on to seventy-four, grand chronicler of all these 'luckless men'; and he, as Dorothy Wellesley once observed, looked as if he had never enjoyed a good day's health in his life.

Mortality and melancholy marked the poetry of this period. Dowson, in his later poem *A Last Word*, writes what is clearly a requiem, a swan-song for a group attitude.

[1] 'The Tragic Generation' (*The Trembling of the Veil*)

Let us go hence: the night is now at hand;
  The day is overworn, the birds all flown;
  And we have reaped the crops the gods have sown:
Despair and death; deep darkness o'er the the land,
Broods like an owl; we cannot understand
  Laughter or tears, for we have only known
  Surpassing vanity: vain thoughts alone
Have driven our perverse and aimless band.

Let us go hence, somewhere strange and cold,
  To Hollow Lands where just men and unjust
  Find end of labour, where's rest for the old,
Freedom to all from love and fear and lust.
Twine our torn hands! O pray the earth enfold
Our life-sick hearts and turn them into dust.[1]

What was the reason for this vast pervading sadness?

III

DURING the last sixty years we have become so accustomed to think of tragedy as something politically imposed from outside—from war, oppression, and persecution—that we may incline to doubt the validity of Yeats' description of his colleagues of the 'nineties as 'the tragic generation'. For us, it is war that appointed two young generations to play the role of tragic heroes; and to us the young men of those earlier years seemed to enjoy an enviable position: heirs to security and peace. The Boer storm which shook the decade at its end was responsible for no such mortality rate amongst artists and men-of-letters as those of the 1914 and 1939 wars. Unlike

[1] *Decorations* (1900)

the Spanish affair, the Boer War was not an intellectual's war.

To begin, then, to understand the fate which somehow involved these men of the 'nineties, we have to adapt our idea of tragedy to fit a quite dissimilar situation. The two key words most often bandied are 'decadence' and 'degeneration'. The second term had been employed as the title for a book which Max Nordau published in 1895. The author, an artistically insensitive German, with a pseudo-scientific lack of humour, believed that from the time of Wagner and the Pre-Raphaelites European culture was the product of sick men. He diagnosed, in elaborate terms, a state of neurasthenia in the arts. Saintsbury, that hard-hitting no-nonsense Scot found 'too much of [Nordau's] book a silly . . . exaggeration, not at all ill-exemplifying the very weaknesses he discussed'.[1] Bernard Shaw, provoked by the book into replying with his own work *The Sanity of Art* (1895), described Nordau's theory as 'at bottom, nothing but the familiar delusion that the world is going to the dogs'. There is no doubt that Nordau's label, stuck by him on to all and sundry, represented no objective approach. Yet even so, the pathological element is to be reckoned with when dealing with these poets. We shall note this element when we come to look at their individual lines. For the moment, we might say, that one aspect of 'decadence' is a pursuit of intensity beyond the strength of the organism.

Yeats, in seeking to solve the mystery of 'the tragic generation', appears to have entertained this notion at least once. 'Perhaps', he wrote, 'our form of lyric, our insistence upon emotion . . . gathered together overwrought, unstable men.' The moment after, he doubts this conjecture: 'I remember that the first to go out of his mind had no lyrical gift, and that we valued him mainly because he seemed a witty man of the world.'[2]

'I have never', he tells us, 'found a full explanation of

[1] *The Bookman*, New York (1895)
[2] 'The Tragic Generation' (*The Trembling of the Veil*)

that tragedy.'[1] His most original hints at a solution interpret it in cultural terms. Part of this interpretation has to do with the greater focussing of the poet's mind on purely aesthetic elements. 'When Edmund Spenser', he tells us, 'described the islands of Phaedria and of Acrasia he aroused the indignation of Lord Burleigh . . . and Lord Burleigh was in the right if morality were our only object. In these islands certain qualities of beauty, certain forms of sensuous loveliness were separated from all general purposes of life, as they had not been hitherto in European literature. . . . I think that the movement of our thought has more and more so separated certain images and regions of the mind, and that these images grow in beauty as they grow in sterility. Shakespeare leaned, as it were, even as craftsmen, upon the general fate of men and nations, had about him the excitement of the playhouse; and all poets . . . until our age came, and when it came almost all, had some propaganda or traditional doctrine to give companionship with their fellows.'[2] The 'nineties dispensed with this companionship. They worked in a solitude of private feelings, removed from emotions of national public life. In this, they were thrown back upon themselves, on resources psychologically insufficient.

> What part in the world can the artist have,
> Who has awakened from the common dream,
> But dissipation and despair?

inquires Yeats[3] knowing how in the last two so many of 'the tragic generation found their answer'.

Intellectually, he inclines to put the blame on Walter Pater. No work of prose was more admired by Yeats than *Marius, the Epicurean*; and yet, he confesses 'I began to wonder if it or the attitude of mind of which it was the noblest expression, had not caused the disaster of my friends. It taught us to walk upon a rope tightly stretched

[1] 'The Tragic Generation' (*The Trembling of the Veil*)
[2] Ibid.
[3] Ibid.

through serene air, and we were left to keep our feet upon a swaying rope in a storm.'[1]

Pater's dangerous doctrines had been broached, of course, in his first book *The Renaissance* (1873). There, he at least came near to substituting sensation for wisdom as the wise man's ultimate aim. Experience, in and for itself, not the fruit of experience was what he recommended. 'The theory or idea or system which requires of us the sacrifice of any part of this experience, in consideration of some interest into which we cannot enter, or some abstract theory we have not identified with ourselves, or of what is only conventional has no real claim upon us.'[2]

Unlike the thinkers of Balliol who were busy proclaiming a public philosophy, Pater's teaching was morbidly subjective. This cult of intensity—namely, that success in life consisted of burning always with a 'hard gem-like flame'—carried with it two corollaries, adopted by the poets of the 'nineties. Both of these were persuasively expressed, both went enveloped in the beauty of pathos.

The first was the notion that life is constituted of flux and that wisdom consists in accepting the fact. 'Not to discriminate every moment some passionate attitude in those about us, and in the very brilliancy of their gifts some tragic dividing of forces on their ways is, on this short day of frost and sun, to sleep before evening.'[3]

The pathos of transcience is written across the poetry of the 'nineties. Predominantly, in Yeats' words, it is the expression of men 'whose hearts perish every moment, and whose bodies melt away like a sigh'.[4]

The second corollary is the idea of the inevitable solitariness of the individual. 'Experience', Pater declares, 'is ringed round for each one of us by that thick wall of personality through which no real voice has ever pierced on its way to us, or from us to that which we can only

[1] Ibid.

[2] *The Renaissance: Studies in Art & Poetry*, Walter Pater (1873)

[3] Ibid.

[4] 'Rosa Alchemica' (*The Secret Rose*) W. B. Yeats (1897)

conjecture to be without. Every one of these impressions is the impression of the individual in his isolation, each mind keeping as a solitary prisoner its own dream of the world.'[1] This privately enclosed impressionism (a word we shall have much trafficking with later) is a characteristic of 'nineties poetry. Usually, it is nothing more than a drifting flock of images, but sometimes as in the Epilogue to Arthur Symons' *London Nights* (1895) it attains to the dignity of philosophic statement.

Credo

Each, in himself, his hour to be and cease
  Endures alone, but who of men shall dare
  Sole with himself, his single burden bear,
All the long day until the night's release?
Yet ere night falls, and the last shadows close,
  This labour of himself is each man's lot;
  All he has gained of earth shall be forgot,
Himself he leaves behind him when he goes.
If he has any valiancy within,
  If he has made his life his very own,
  If he has loved or labour'd, and has known
A strenuous virtue, or a strenuous sin;
Then, being dead, his life was not all vain,
  For he has saved what most desire to lose,
  And he has chosen what the few must choose,
Since life, once lived, shall not return again.
For of our time we lose so large a part
  In serious trifles, and so oft let slip
  The wine of every moment, at the lip
Its moment, and the moment of the heart.
We are awake so little on the earth,
  And we shall sleep so long, and rise so late,
  If there is any knocking at that gate
Which is the gate of death, the gate of birth.

[1] *The Renaissance: Studies in Art & Poetry*, Walter Pater

IV

LOOKING back to those *fin-de-siècle* years from the changed climate of 1914, Yeats wrote his great verse epitaph on 'the tragic generation'. Speaking of those 'Companions of the Rhymers Club . . . poets from whom I learned my trade',[1] he recalled both their tragic lives and their artistic heroism.

> You had to face your ends when young—
> 'Twas wine or women, or some curse—
> But never made a poorer song
> That you might have a heavier purse,
> Nor gave loud service to a cause
> That you might have a troup of friends.
> You kept the Muses' sterner laws,
> And unrepenting faced your ends.

The Rhymers Club was, indeed, the chief distillery of 'nineties poetry. Through its two anthologies it gave the tyro poets a hearing, providing them with a common cause and the conversation of their kind. Founded in the winter of 1891, the group lasted for three years, meeting 'in an upper room with a sanded floor in an ancient eating-house in the Strand [sic] called "The Cheshire Cheese" '.[2] Yeats recalls the part he played in the inception of the Club with Ernest Rhys, a Welsh ex-mining engineer, poet, editor, translator. 'I had', he tells us, 'already met most of the poets of my generation. I had said to the editor of a series of shilling reprints, who had set me to compile tales of the Irish fairies, "I am growing jealous of other poets and we will all grow jealous of each other unless we know each other and so feel a share in each other's triumphs." '[3]

[1] 'The Grey Rock' (*Responsibilities*) (1914)
[2] 'Four Years 1887–1891' (*The Trembling of the Veil*)
[3] Ibid.

If it was this sentiment which led to the meetings and readings of the Club, the idea of producing an anthology together probably derives from the following letter: 'Thank you', wrote Edmund Gosse, already established as a critic, to Ernest Rhys who had sent him a sheaf of poems, 'for letting me read your very beautiful lyric "A London Rose" . . . I wish I could suggest something sensible about the publishing of your book. It seems more difficult than ever to sell verse. I have been trying to find a publisher for Arthur Symons, alas, without success. It seems to me that it would be rather a good plan if four or five of the very best of you young poets would club together to produce a volume, a new Parnassus, and so give the reading public a chance of making your acquaintance.'[1]

Many accounts have been given of the Club's make-up and meetings. Yeats, as often, is picturesque but inaccurate as to names and dates. The most conscientious and vivid record is that left by Victor Plarr, himself a Rhymer, in the story of his friend *Ernest Dowson, 1888–1897*. Among the list of members and guests these names of importance are included: Lionel Johnson, Ernest Dowson, Arthur Symons, John Davidson, Richard Le Gallienne, John Gray, Francis Thompson, and Oscar Wilde.

Despite the slim churchwarden pipes and the tankards of beer set out on the tables, the Rhymers Club, according to Symons, was 'not quite a satisfactory kind of cénacle'.[2] Fresh from the greater freedom of Paris which he so often visited, Symons could not help but notice the inhibited air of embarrassed good breeding which these occasions sometimes wore. 'In England', he wrote, 'art has to be protected not only against the world, but against one's self and one's fellow artist, by a kind of affected modesty which is the Englishman's natural pose, half pride and half self-distrust.'[3]

Yeats also reminisced on the bug of English over-

[1] *Letters from Limbo* by Ernest Rhys (1936)
[2] 'Ernest Dowson' (*Studies in Prose and Verse*) by Arthur Symons
[3] Ibid.

politeness. 'Conversation constantly dwindled into "Do you like so-and-so's last book?" "No, I prefer, the book before it." '[1] Had it not been for its Irish members, he believed the Club would not have survived its few difficult months. Dress, too, was unexceptional. No other members of the Club, except Le Gallienne, who wore a loose tie, and Symons, who had an Inverness cape that was quite new and almost fashionable, would have shown himself for the world in any costume but 'that of an English gentleman'.[2]

Behind this correct exterior was artistic dedication and a hint of riot.

From habits of noctambulism at New College, Oxford, and a state of insomnia which so often plagued him, Lionel Johnson had fled to whiskey. But with the passing of the short tally of his years the jug of 'Glengary whiskey between two open books: *Les Fleurs du Mal* and *Leaves of Grass*'[3] grew to become 'a craving that made every atom of his body cry out'.[4] As early as 1893 he was writing to his flat-mate and landlord Mackmurdo, promising to take the pledge if he were allowed to remain in the house. Attempting to guide friends to the door, late at night with a lighted candle, he had taken to tumbling and falling about to the danger of all beneath the same roof. The statements in his letter, as Iain Fletcher shows, point to self-contradiction and deception: 'As long as it depends upon my own will I am quite hopeless. . . . Medically speaking, I am not hopelessly given up to drink. . . . It will be quite easy with the pledge.'[5] At the time of his death in 1902, he was drinking two pints of whiskey every twenty-four hours. At Winchester he had been a leading member of a homosexual circle. Since his conversion to the Roman faith in 1891, he appeared to have repressed all outward practices, but the strain of keeping this tendency in check added to the tension and burden of his life.

[1] 'Four Years 1887–1891' (*The Trembling of the Veil*)
[2] Ibid.
[3] *The Middle Span* by George Santayana (1947)
[4] 'The Tragic Generation' (*The Trembling of the Veil*)
[5] *The Complete Poems of Lionel Johnson*, ed. by Iain Fletcher (1953)

Dowson, meanwhile, come down from Oxford, was treading a parallel path where the bonfire at the end was quite as much in view as any incidental primroses *en route*. The lungs of this young man with 'the face of a demoralized Keats'[1] were touched already with the phthisis which destroyed him. In Soho, he had fallen in love with Adelaide Foltinowicz, the daughter of a restaurant keeper. His suit did not prosper and a morbid shyness withheld him from declaring his feelings to the girl. Three hours away from this unresponsive idol, the whole nature of the man changed. 'Under the influence of drink', recalls Arthur Symons, 'he became literally insane, certainly quite unresponsible. He fell into furious and unreasoning passions; a vocabulary unknown to him at other times sprang up like a whirlwind; he seemed always about to commit some act of absurd violence. Along with that forgetfulness came other memories. As long as he was conscious of himself, there was but one woman for him in the world, and for her he had an infinite tenderness and an infinite respect. When that face faded from him, he saw all the other faces and he saw no more difference than between sheep and sheep.'[2]

In 1897 Adelaide married the German waiter who worked at her parents' restaurant. Dowson's mother and father committed suicide; he dying with poison, she with a rope. The poet of 'wine and women and song'[3] now became the singer of 'Love's Aftermath'[4] as can be seen from the following poem:

> The fire is out, and spent the warmth thereof
> (This is the end of every song man sings!)
> The golden wine is drunk, the dregs remain,
> Bitter as wormwood and as salt as pain;
> And health and hope have gone the way of love.
> Into the drear oblivion of lost things.
> Ghosts go along with us until the end;

[1] 'Ernest Dowson' (*Studies in Prose and Verse*) by Arthur Symons
[2] Ibid.
[3] 'Villanelle of the Poets' Road' (*Decorations*) by Ernest Dowson (1900)
[4] 'Beyond' (*Decorations*) by Ernest Dowson

This was a mistress, this, perhaps, a friend.
With pale, indifferent eyes, we sit and wait
For the dropt curtain and the closing gate:
This is the end of all the songs man sings.[1]

Other images of fevered living came to characterise the decade: Symons taking hashish with ladies of the ballet, in the company of Dowson and J. A. Symonds in his rooms in Fountain Court in the Temple (the experiment did not work, however—'it ended in what should have been its first symptom, immoderate laughter');[2] Yeats taking hashish in Paris, while pursuing his occult studies with 'some followers of the eighteenth-century mystic Saint-Martin'[3] (this time with more effect—'at one in the morning and some are dancing');[4] Beardsley, the period's malefic illustrator, arriving with a tarty young woman at Yeats' rooms in Fountain Court, a little after breakfast and slightly drunk after his dismissal as art editor of *The Yellow Book* ('He puts his hand upon the wall and stares into a mirror, "Yes, yes, I look like a Sodomite," which he certainly did not',[5] or 'propped up on a chair in the middle of the room [at his publisher's Leonard Smithers] grey and exhausted, leaving the party to go into another room and spit blood.'[6]

The Decadence would seem to have had a physiology and psychology all its own.

Against these glimpses of indulgence and debauch must be set other images of positive import: Johnson, fasting before Communion, forcing himself to lie awake all night, most likely reading the Early Fathers, never daring to relax, since 'in some unguarded instant, struggling from sleep, the old enemy might wake with him and his fast be broken by the familiar sound of liquid tinkling in a glass';[7]

[1] 'Dregs' (*Decorations*) by Ernest Dowson
[2] 'Ernest Dowson' (*Studies in Prose and Verse*) by Arthur Symons. (See also *Arthur Symons: A Critical Biography* by Roger Lhombreaud (1963))
[3] 'The Tragic Generation' (*The Trembling of the Veil*)
[4] Ibid.
[5] Ibid.
[6] Ibid.
[7] *The Complete Poems of Lionel Johnson*, ed. by Iain Fletcher

Dowson, for all his heart-ache and sickness, living on a pittance in Brittany and working away at translating Voltaire and Zola, his 'care over English prose [being] like that of a Frenchman writing his own language with the respect which Frenchmen pay to French';[1] Beardsley, ignoring the handkerchief red with blood to draw the curtains against the daylight and light the candles within the room since he often drew best by artificial light; Symons, 'a scholar in music-halls as another man might be a Greek scholar'[2] returning late from the Empire or the Alhambra, only to pernoctate with George Moore the post-midnight precincts of King's Bench Walk and Fountain Court, tired but talking tirelessly of 'symbolism or gesture. Or was it symbolism in rhythm . . . ?'[3]—Moore couldn't decide which.

In most of these men was a dedicatory passion; a belief in something, a striving towards it. Yet present in each was an antithetical self—a force leading not to attention and achievement, but one which dispersed the concentrative effort; and against it the powers of resistance were too small.

Perhaps the quality singularly lacking in both the lives and work of these men was a strain of toughness, of coarseness even. Yeats, watching Alfred Jarry's symbolist-expressionist farce *Ubu Roi* in company with Symons at the end of the century, seemed to feel the art of the Rhymers judged and sentenced by some harsh new manifestation:

> The players are supposed to be dolls, toys, marionettes, and now they are all hopping like wooden frogs, and I can see for myself that the chief personage, who is some kind of king, carries for sceptre a brush of the kind that we use to clean a closet . . . That night at the Hotel Corneille I am very sad. . . . I say, 'After Stéphane Mallarmé, after Paul Verlaine, after Gustave Moreau, after Puvis de

[1] 'Ernest Dowson (*Studies in Prose and Verse*) by Arthur Symons
[2] *Letters to the New Island*, Harvard (1924)
[3] *Ave* by George Moore (1911)

Chevannes, after our own verse, after all our subtle colour and nervous rhythm, after the faint mixed tints of Conder, what more is possible? After us the Savage God.'[1]

Ahead lay surrealism, Wyndham Lewis, D. H. Lawrence.

V

BUT this is to anticipate the Rhymers' story. Their first anthology appearing in March 1892, they all had this brief respite of years in which to work.

The date of the first *Book of the Rhymers Club* is itself significant. In the same year, seven months later, Tennyson—the star Victorian poet—died. Great and popular laureate, as he was, to these young men Tennyson represented the triumph of a mixed and middle-class art. With the famed practitioner of this old mode of poetry dead, the way was open for a fresh style in verse.

In place of a poetry of ideas, we were now to have poetry for poetry's sake. The Rhymer figures deliberately chose to emulate the pure art of fine minor poets rather than the often impure work of major ones. In his 'Toast' to the Rhymers, printed in their first *Book*, Ernest Rhys acknowledged these new adherences:

> As once Rare Ben and Herrick
>   Set older Fleet Street mad,
> With wit not esoteric,
> And laughter that was lyric,
>   And roystering rhymes and glad.

[1] 'The Tragic Generation' (*The Trembling of the Veil*)

As they, we drink defiance
  Tonight to all but Rhyme,
And most of all to Science,
And all such skins of lions
  That hide the ass of Time.

In this century of Science and Progress, little respect was accorded to the former by these poets. Yeats tells us how he 'detested' Huxley and Tyndall, feeling that they had deprived him of 'the simple-minded religion of my childhood'.[1] Along with science as a demonological subject, in Yeats' mind, went Ibsenism, comedy, objectivity, and G. B. Shaw. 'I had a nightmare', Yeats wrote of the latter, 'that I was haunted by a sewing machine, that clicked and shone, but the incredible thing was that the machine smiled, smiled perpetually.'[2]

Among the Bohemian élite of the Rhymers, progressive opinion was often unwelcomed. Symons found colourful romantic reasons against the Suffragette movement; while Dowson showed how wide was the gulf between himself and the affairs of the age when he said that, for himself, he was most led to fear an invasion by the Red Indians.[3]

Greatest of this company as he was later to become, Yeats in the first half of the 'nineties was way behind many of them on points of inventiveness, modernity, and technique. 'Dowson, Johnson . . . or Symons,' he admitted, 'had what I still lacked, conscious deliberate craft, and what I must lack always, scholarship.'[4] 'What I wanted from the poets of the 'nineties', T.S. Eliot has told us, 'was what they did not have in common with the pre-Raphaelites, but what was new and original in their work.'[5] There was, at this time, little beyond Pre-Raphaelitism in Yeats' poetry, the clear fixed colours of the earlier poets merging beneath an obscuring Celtic

[1] 'Four Years 1887–1891' (*The Trembling of the Veil*)
[2] 'The Tragic Generation' (*The Trembling of the Veil*)
[3] *Ernest Dowson: 1888–1897* (1914) by Victor Plarr
[4] 'Modern Poetry' (*Essays and Introductions*)
[5] *John Davidson: A Selection of his Poems*, Preface by T.S. Eliot (1961)

twilight. Some few shades of Spenser and Shelley, 'a fardel of old [Irish] tales',[1] the recollection of certain folk-songs, and a dominant emotional immaturity—such was Yeats' stock-in-trade in those days. Even so, such a poem as *The Lamentation of the Old Pensioner* has some of the aggressive naturalness we associate with his later poems:

> I spit into the face of Time
> That has transfigured me.[2]

Yeats' contemporary instructor was Symons, a great importer of French styles into England. He was himself a poet of many poses, but his verse does succeed in delineating 'the décor which is the town equivalent of the great natural décor of fields and hills'.[3] Urbane, in the original and derivative sense, his poetry naturalises aspects of 'the variable, most human, and yet most factitious town landscape'.[4] Symons' poetry, along with that of Laforgue, is behind T. S. Eliot's early compositions: his *Preludes* and *The Love Song of J. Alfred Prufrock.* 'I also had a good many dingy urban images to reveal',[5] Eliot has told us. It is even easy to see how

> The feverish room and that white bed,
> The tumbled skirts upon a chair,
> The novel flung half-open where
> Hat, hair-pins, puffs, and paints are spread[6]

of Symons becomes the décor and belongings of 'the typist home at tea-time' from Eliot's disseminated masterpiece *The Waste Land:*

> Out of the window perilously spread
> Her drying combinations touched by the sun's last rays,
> On the divan are piled (at night her bed)
> Stockings, slippers, camisoles, and stays.[7]

[1] 'Four Years 1887–1891' (*The Trembling of the Veil*)
[2] *The Rose* (1893)
[3] *Silhouettes* (2nd edition) by Arthur Symons (1896)
[4] Ibid.
[5] *John Davidson: A Selection of his Poems,* Preface by T.S. Eliot
[6] 'White Heliotrope' (*London Nights*) (1895)
[7] *Collected Poems 1909–1935*

Yeats spoke of Symons as 'a writer who has carried further than most . . . that revolt against the manifold, the impersonal, the luxuriant, and the eternal'[1]—by which four qualities he refers to the moralising, sermonising verse of the Victorians with its descriptive, idealistic, over-literary bias. Victorian poetry was often an art of argument: for the 'nineties, all abstract issues in verse were justified only as expressive instruments of subjective feeling. 'Literature', wrote Yeats in 1895, 'differs from explanatory and scientific writing in being wrought about a mood, or a community of moods . . . and if it uses argument, theory, erudition, observation, and seems to grow hot in assertion or denial, it does so merely to make us partakers at the banquet of the moods.'[2]

Mood was a key word with the critics of the 'nineties in the way that *temperament* had been the *Open Sesame* in Pater's writing. Symons' poetics bear indeed a striking resemblance to those of D. H. Lawrence, who said that he sought not 'the infinite or the eternal' but 'the incarnate moment . . . the immediate present, the Now'.[3] Place beside this Symons' description of his own poetry as 'a sincere attempt to render a particular mood which has once been mine, and to render it as if, for the moment, there was no other mood for me in the world',[4] and the insistence upon the present—the exclusive personal present—in both these poets is remarkable. How well, too, D. H. Lawrence's description of his own verse as 'unrestful, ungraspable'[5] applies to the elusive verse of Symons. A 'Herrick of the Music-Halls', as he was called, he pursued an aesthetic of the fleeting, the fine fugitive beauty of transcience. His is a poetry of mutability, an art of whatever flickers mysteriously into attraction at the very moment, almost, of its exit:

[1] *Bookman*, London (April 1897)
[2] 'The Moods' (*Essays and Introductions*)
[3] *New Poems*, New York (1920)
[4] *Studies in Prose and Verse* (1904)
[5] *New Poems*, New York

Her face's wilful flash and glow
Turned all its light upon my face
One bright delirious moment's space,
And then she passed . . .[1]

Or take this even more abbreviated morse impressionism —a poem on the coming of the London dark—which Ernest Rhys quotes as characteristic of the poet:

Next moment! Ah! it was—was not!
I heard the chilliness of the street.
Night came. The stars had not forgot.
The moonlight fell about my feet.[2]

Without the range of Symons, but with a greater purity of artistic intention was Ernest Dowson. Translator of Verlaine, as were others of these poets, he set before himself the precept of 'la musique/Avant toutes choses'[3]— 'Music before all things'—possessing, in fact, little talent for anything save music. 'He used the commonplaces of poetry frankly' and 'sang one tune over and over again'.[4] The song was a sad one, and today we regret that the poet lacked wit in his unrequited love. At his best, however, he does achieve a fastidious economy of self-pity which, serving rather to preserve than dissipate the obsession, results in an elegant confessional statement, such as we find in the poem headed 'O Mors! quam amara est memoria tua homini pacem habenti in substantiis suis.'[5]

It is the very slenderness of Dowson's resources—a 'pure lyric gift, unweighted or unballasted by any other quality of mind or emotion'[6]—which gave him his real distinction as a poet. His art is as far removed as is possible from the 'omniorum' poetry of the great Victorians. It is so thin, so fragile, it is hardly there, and yet that thinness conserves its purity.

The poetry of Lionel Johnson, beside that of these other two, seems a stiff and formal thing. It lacks both Dowson's

[1] 'On the Heath' (*Silhouettes*) (1892)
[2] *Everyman Remembers* by Ernest Rhys (1931)
[3] 'Art poetique' [4] 'Ernest Dowson' (*Studies in Prose and Verse*)
[5] *Verses* (1896) [6] 'Ernest Dowson' (*Studies in Prose and Verse*)

lyric simplicity—the semblance of the heart uttering its feelings—and Symons' sophisticated inquiry. There is little adventurousness, little inventiveness in his verses; and they are burdened by a greater residue of Victorian diction than those of the other poets.

An essentially lonely man, he developed in his life a ritual of friendship to which the individual dedication of his several poems bears witness. It is certainly the intimate friendly tone—of a friend with a love of niceties and manners—which introduces an element of the easy and familiar into such poems as *Plato in London* and *Oxford Nights*. To Johnson, books were friends, and most of his friends were bookish. His old-fashionedness in literary etiquette was, in fact, a conscious reaction to both Decadent emancipation and to Victorian Philistinism. The latter fashion he parodied in a handful of brief pieces, of which *A Decadent's Lyric* is the best. His short story *Incurable* contains, among others, the following little skit:

> Ah, day by swift malignant day,
> Life vanishes in vanity:
> Whilst I, life's phantom victim, play
> The music of my misery.
> Draw near, ah dear delaying Death!
> Draw near, and silence my sad breath![1]

As Johnson's young poet in the story remarks, 'It was good, but Shakespeare and Keats, little as he could comprehend why, had done better.'

Johnson's own poetry seeks to revive memorials of 'a gracious age'.[2] (Like Dowson, he was a member of the White Rose League which commemorates the Stuarts.) His art is that of the born bookman, more a matter of libraries than of life. Even so, to read him today is still an education in manners. And when his classic control finds some familiar subject on which it can work, the resultant poem has charm, ease and grace:

[1] *The Complete Poems of Lionel Johnson*, ed. Iain Fletcher
[2] 'The Age of a Dream' (*Poems*) (1895)

On me and mine
Clear candlelights in quiet shine:
My fire lives yet! nor have I done
With *Smollett*, nor with *Richardson*.[1]

No poet who frequented the Rhymers Club can have differed more from Johnson than the Scot John Davidson. To him, with his contentious nature and native pleasure in strenuous thinking, the refinements of these poets seemed 'an effeminate pedantry'.[2] Argument at the Rhymers was out. 'Criticism founded upon general ideas', as Yeats observed, 'was itself an impurity.'[3] For him, its members lacked 'blood and guts.'[4] In Mallarmé's phrase, they wished to keep 'a little cigarette smoke between [themselves] and the world'.[5] Temperamentally, Davidson was closer to the poetry of Henley and Kipling with its rough-and-tumble realism and its 'commitment'.

T. S. Eliot has recorded the impact which Davidson's poem *Thirty Bob a Week* made upon him as a freshman.[6] But the work is marred by a combination of lively colloquial idiom with language drawn from evolutionary philosophy. Johnson noted that 'his beauty and his strength were not in perfect accord . . . [and that] Davidson's work often required a last refining touch to transfigure it into a very wonderful thing'.[7] This touch is absent in most of his pieces, and his two 'perfections', *In Romney Marsh* and *A Runnable Stag* took to the Georgian verse with its genuine or factitious rustic gusto.

The last name of importance here is that of Oscar Wilde. The senior of these poets in age and reputation, Wilde was not a member of the Rhymers Club, although he had attended as a guest. His first volume of poems had appeared in 1881, and his style in general was lush and prolix—a kind of Victorian baroque. There were, how-

[1] 'Oxford Nights (*Poems*) (1895)
[2] 'The Tragic Generation' (*The Trembling of the Veil*)
[3] Ibid. [4] Ibid.
[5] *The Symbolist Movement in Modern Literature* by Arthur Symons (1899)
[6] *John Davidson: A Selection of his Poems*, Preface by T. S. Eliot
[7] *The Complete Poems of Lionel Johnson*, ed. Iain Fletcher

ever, exceptions to this. *The Harlot's House*, written in tercets, has directness, tempo, economy which few of the poets of the 'nineties could equal.

> We caught the tread of dancing feet,
> We loitered down the moonlit street,
> And stopped beneath the harlot's house.
>
> Inside, above the din and fray,
> We heard the loud musicians play
> The 'Treues Liebes Herz' of Strauss.

Plagiarising Gautier and Whistler, he produced a number of poems which he spoke of as 'harmonies' or 'impressions'. These compositions are skilful arrangements of the poet's visual data—made up by someone with a window-dresser's eye. They look towards Imagism, and possibly influenced Arthur Symons:

> The yellow fog came creeping down
> The bridges, till the houses' walls
> Seemed changed to shadows and St. Paul's
> Loomed like a bubble o'er the town.[1]

But these pieces belong to the 'eighties, the years during which he wrote nearly all his verse. In 1895 had come his disgrace, and in 1898 there was published a work in a new manner, *The Ballad of Reading Gaol*. Wilde, in his suffering was still the actor. Impressive as it is, *The Ballad* is marked with histrionic affectation. Parallelism, repetition, antitheses liberally bestrew its verses. Its pitch is often over-strained; the declaiming voice is too frequently heard. Even so, there are passages where a new intimacy of tone is present. And these passages, in the speaking voice, are the best thing in all Wilde's poetry. Their natural quietness is the more penetrating:

> I never saw a man who looked
> With such a wistful eye
> Upon that little tent of blue
> Which prisoners call the sky.

[1] 'Impression du Matin' (*Collected Poems*) (1908)

When all his rhetoric was hushed, Wilde spoke superbly with a still small voice.

VI

TO speak of the poets of the 'nineties as essentially modern might appear a paradox. That *fin-de-siècle* decade, with its contrived naughtiness, may seem to many a period-piece epoch. Its ethics were largely a pose, its sentiments part of a decorative pattern. The 'nineties has been called the 'Beardsley Period', but to think of the art and literature of that era as consisting solely, in the illustrator's own words, of 'strange hermaphrodite creatures wandering about in Pierrot costumes'[1] is to take the part for the whole. Speaking of his early days at Harvard, T. S. Eliot has told us that 'the poets of the 'nineties . . . were the only poets . . . who at that period of history seemed to have anything to offer me as a beginner . . . One was Arthur Symons . . . another was Ernest Dowson . . . and the third was [John] Davidson . . . from these men I got the idea that one could write poetry in an English such as one would speak oneself. A colloquial idiom. There was a spoken rhythm in some of these poems.'[2]

This emancipation from '*tutti frutti* Tennysonian afflatus'[3] and an all-too-conventional and bookish grandiloquence was the English counterpart of Verlaine's decision to take rhetoric and wring its neck. The French poet did indeed visit London, lecturing at Barnard's Inn and Oxford, as the guest of Arthur Symons in 1893. 'Music before all things . . . and, as far as that goes, choose rather the imperfect accord . . . the twilight tune where the precise

[1] *John Lane & the 'Nineties* by J. Lewis May (1936)
[2] *John Davidson: A Selection of his Poems*, Preface by T. S. Eliot.
[3] Ibid. Maurice Lindsay's 'Introduction'

and the indefinite join hands. Let your poem be a gay adventure . . . Fresh with the morning smells of mint and thyme. And all the rest is literature', Verlaine had written quizzically in *Art Poetique*, the manifesto of a new verbal freedom, which was also, of course, a new discipline.

All too few of the English poets were able to lift their diction out of the rut of Victorian heaviness.

> The touches of man's modern speech
> Perplex her unacquainted tongue

complained Francis Thompson in *The Singer saith of his Song*.[1] Lionel Johnson described the style of his second book of poems as 'hopelessly in the would-be austere and hieratic manner'.[2] This regulation rhetoric of the nineteenth century certainly took some breaking down; but here and there, from time to time, a number of the more forward poets made the break-through into a style more simple, precise, and urbane. Arthur Symons, critical spokesman of the era, mapped out the new direction in a magazine article in 1893. Linking together the gospels of Impressionism, Symbolism, and Decadence, he spoke of 'this endeavour after a perfect truth to one's impression, to one's intuition . . . [which] has brought with it, in its revolt from ready-made impressions and conclusions, a revolt from the ready-made of language, from the bondage of traditional form, of a form become rigid'.[3]

The poets of the 'nineties reacted in fact against the pomposities of convention in general. The reign of the ponderous sage, of Ruskin and Carlyle, was over. If Pater was venerated by these young men it was because his Cause was that of Art and because he taught that 'a certain shade of unconcern'[4] is the mark of a complete culture in the handling of great issues and abstract questions. Victorianism, with its top-heavy excess of seriousness was on its way out. Matthew Arnold's 'seriousness' might well

[1] *The Poems of Francis Thompson, 1913*
[2] *The Complete Poems of Lionel Johnson* (1953)
[3] 'The Decadent Movement in Literature' (*Dramatis Personae*) (1925)
[4] 'Coleridge' (*Appreciations*) (1889)

by himself be described as 'high'—but 'high' and 'heavy' are not the same thing, and Arnold's airy skirmishings with the British philistine, on behalf of sweetness and light, were conducted with a cavalier nonchalance and irony. With Pater and Arnold, then, as mentors the poets of the 'nineties renounced the Abyss of the Ethical Commonplace which so often darkly beckoned the Victorian masters.

In the 'nineties, Victorian middle-class verse gave way to an aristocratic poetic. Manners took precedence over morality. Irony and wit replaced philosophizing. As Yeats was later to comment, 'Tennyson . . . Browning had admitted so much psychology, science, and moral fervour.'[1]

VII

THE 'nineties poetry which interests us most today is not that aspect of its verse which we find reflected in A. J. A. Symons' *An Anthology of the 'Nineties* published in 1928. This is the 'nineties of Baudelaire—of Baudelaire in English, reflected and distorted through the wrappings of Victorian rhetoric. Most of the turgidity of language, the over-heated thought and feeling discoverable in the 'nineties poets derives from that element of the Time-Spirit.

Swinburne has been a great praiser of Baudelaire; and Swinburne was admired and imitated by the poets of the 'nineties. Baudelaire and Swinburne, in conjunction, constituted a formidable influence. Dowson and Johnson were men with Latin, and the severer economies of Horace may have protected them from the fuller ravagement of a tropical rhetoric. Even so, Dowson, had he lived, 'could

[1] 'Modern Poetry' (*Essays and Introductions*)

only have echoed himself; and probably it would have been the least essential part of himself; his obligation to Swinburne, always evident, increasing as his own inspiration failed him'.[1] And there were other poets who failed to make full contact with their inspiration because of the Baudelaire-Swinburnian idiom, approved by the age, which came between.

But there was another side to the 'nineties, centred about a third influence—that of the poet Verlaine. Lecturing on 'Contemporary French Poetry' in London, he had met the younger poets at 'The Crown', 'a semi-literary tavern near Leicester Square, chosen for its convenient position between two stage-doors'.[2] From Verlaine, the 'nineties poets began to learn the lesson of insouciance, of lightly wooing back the spoken word into the context of the all-too-literary. Kipling had brought the colloquial back, but with such a bump that the older graces were thrust through the bottom of the poem. What the 'nineties poets sought, and sometimes achieved, and what Verlaine himself offered, was a new reconciliation between the written and the spoken word.

Often defeated in this purpose, often maintaining it for a short passage only (sometimes no longer than a phrase or so), the 'nineties poets opened the way for Eliot and Pound and those who came after. Urbanity, lightness, irony and wit, the *double entendre*, and the verbal shrug, the precise statement, and the pure melodic line—the 'nineties poets acquaint us with these.

Nothing can better illustrate the tempo and techniques of the two poetries—the Victorian and the old, the 'nineties and the new—than a comparison of this passage of Tennyson with two stanzas from the verse of the 'nineties.

> One walk'd between his wife and child,
> With measured footstep firm and mild,
> And now and then he gravely smiled.

[1] 'Ernest Dowson' (*Studies in Prose and Verse*) by Arthur Symons
[2] *Memories of a Victorian* by E. Jepson (1933)

The prudent partner of his blood
Lean'd on him, faithful, gentle, good,
Wearing the rose of womanhood.[1]

The Laureate, as always, is felicitous, of course: his lines have balance and choice of diction. But the end result lacks dignity. Thought, sentiment, and wording are unbearably stuffy. 'The prudent partner of his blood'—is it the adjective or the nounal phrase which seems the more affected?

The second passage concerns what befell a certain 'charming cantatrice' as she rested for a moment in the day's heat 'along a path that skirts the wood'.

The gracious boy is at her feet,
  And weighs his courage with his chance;
His fears soon melt in noonday heat.
  The tourist gives a furious glance,
Red as his guide-book grows, moves on, and offers up
    a prayer for France.[2]

Nobody would ever claim this as great poetry, but it has naturalness and tempo. How right—perfectly, ironically right—is the simile chosen for the tourist's complexion: 'red as his guide-book'. The 'prudent partner of his blood' is not a *person* but a circumlocution. 'Red as his guide-book', on the other hand, is the sort of ready colloquialism which refers graphically to a *thing*.

The last stanza from Victor Plarr's exequy for a lady of easy virtue confirms us in our sense of appropriate comment:

Oh, for it would be a pity
  To o'erpraise her or to flout her:
She was wild, and sweet, and witty—
  Let's not say dull things about her.[3]

There is no question of Plarr or Beardsley being anything but minor poets. But in them we have a small skill

[1] 'The Two Voices' (*The Poetical Works of Tennyson*)
[2] *The Three Musicians* by Aubrey Beardsley
[3] 'Epitaphium Citharistriae' (*In the Dorian Mood*) (1896)

used appositely, while Tennyson with all his much fuller resources in the poem quoted is curiously out of key.

The 'nineties note, at its best, may not be sustained beyond a few lines. Yeats, for example, in his famous free rendition of Ronsard can only manage three and a half lines out of four:

> When you are old and gray and full of sleep,
> And nodding by the fire, take down this book,
> And slowly read, and dream of the soft look
> Your eyes had once, and of their shadows deep;[1]

Everything here is right save the last word—the unnatural *literary* position of the adjective *after* the noun. Book-speech was always overtaking the spoken language which these poets were beginning to incorporate in their poems.

Sometimes the imagery of the line is literary and conventional, but redeemed by its stresses which are those of speech:

> Red Rose, proud Rose, sad Rose of all my days![2]

Many minor triumphs of 'nineties poetry derived from its economy of means. Unlike a number of Victorian poets, slowly unwinding their spools of description, these later writers learnt to express themselves *in petto*, to flash an impression upon the reader by almost abbreviated means.

> Night, a grey sky, a ghostly sea,
> The soft beginning of the rain . . .[3]

writes Symons in a nocturne at Dieppe; or, again, of the cathedral at Burgos:

> Miraculous silver-work in stone
> Against the blue miraculous skies[4]

[1] 'When you are old' (*The Rose*) (1893) by W. B. Yeats
[2] 'To the Rose upon the Rood of Time' (*The Rose*)
[3] 'On the Beach' (*Silhouettes*) (1892)
[4] 'At Burgos' (*Silhouettes*)

or of the following amorous recollection:

> In the moonlit room your face,
> Moonlight-coloured, fainting white . . .[1]

Symons' atmospheric effects are produced by means predominantly visual. Johnson, by contrast, a much less compact poet, works through the evocation of an aural impact:

> White Morfydd through the woods
> Went on a moonlight night.[2]

The patterning here of the consonants (w, m, w/w, m, n) skilfully avoids the obvious effects which alliteration and parallelism if too exact can have.

Much has been made of Dowson's addiction to the use of the letter 'v' in verse,[3] but when all is said and done, he, of all the 'nineties poets, has the finest and surest ear. The last line of his poem 'To a Lady Asking Foolish Questions'[4] is a masterpiece of internal near-rhymes:

> I *go* where the wind *blows*, *Chloe*, and
> am not *sorry* at all.[5]

Looking back in 1936, Yeats in a broadcast declared that 'the period from the death of Tennyson until the present moment has, it seems, more good lyric poets than any similar period since the seventeenth century—no great overpowering figures, but many poets who have written some three or four lyrics apiece which may be permanent in our literature'.[6] The virtue of this judgment is in its moderation; and if it should prove prophetic, the poets of the 'nineties will have played their part.

[1] 'Clair de Lune' (*London Nights*) (1895)
[2] 'Sylvan Morfydd' (*The Complete Poems of Lionel Johnson*)
[3] 'Ernest Dowson' (*Studies in Prose and Verse*) by Arthur Symons
[4] *Decorations* (1900) [5] My italics. Ed.
[6] 'Modern Poetry' (*Essays and Introductions*)

Aubrey Beardsley

1872–1898

AUBREY BEARDSLEY was born on 21st August 1872 at Brighton whose Regency remains and associations certainly coloured his own imagination.

The full life of this 'Fra Angelico of Satanism'[1] has yet to be written, though a sufficiency of data exists. In 1937 R. A. Walker edited the letters from *Aubrey Beardsley to Leonard Smithers*[2] his publisher during the last four years of his life. In 1904 Canon John Gray collected and introduced *The Last Letters of Aubrey Beardsley*, written to André Raffalovich, the friend and patron of both these men. In 1898, Arthur Symons published his short monograph *Aubrey Beardsley*, the subject having been art editor to Symons' short-lived periodical *The Savoy*. Holbrook Jackson, Bernard Muddiman, and Osbert Burdett all have chapters on Beardsley in their books on the period;[3] but the fullest account of his life so far written is to be found in Robert Ross's brief study *Aubrey Beardsley* published in 1909.

The rise of this boy whose talents changed the black-and-white art of the world has been many times outlined.

[1] 'Aubrey Beardsley' (*Vision and Design*) by Roger Fry (1920)
[2] First Edition Club (London)
[3] *The Eighteen Nineties* by Holbrook Jackson (1913)
The Men of the Nineties by Bernard Muddiman (1920)
The Beardsley Period by Osbert Burdett (1925)

Employed as a clerk in a London insurance company, he executed his first drawings at night. 'This became a settled habit', William Gaunt tells us. 'Like Huysman's hero he cultivated seclusion. The room had to be darkened before he could start work, and candles lit in two tall ormolu Empire candlesticks.'[1]

His first chance came when he was invited to illustrate the two-volume edition of *Morte d'Arthur* for J. M. Dent in 1893. His appointment as art editor to *The Yellow Book* in 1894 marked the measure of his impact. Henceforth, as Wilde so vividly put it, his 'face like a silver hatchet with grass-green hair'[2] was regularly to be seen in literary and artistic circles. Beardsley was on the top of the wave, enjoying every social occasion, 'always carrying his large, gilt-leather portfolio with the magnificent old, red-lined folio paper'.[3]

Dismissed by the over-cautious John Lane when the scandal of the Wilde trial exploded over London, he was taken on by the publisher Leonard Smithers, whose firm rivalled Lane's Bodley Head as publishers of the *avant-garde*. Arthur Symons tells how he went to Beardsley to ask him to act as art editor to *The Savoy* in 1895, a publication intended by Smithers to out-yellow *The Yellow Book* 'which had by that time ceased to mark a movement and had come to be little more than a publisher's magazine'. 'I forgot', writes Symons, 'exactly when the expulsion of Beardsley from *The Yellow Book* had occurred; it had been sufficiently recent, at all events, to make Beardsley singularly ready to fall in with my project when I went to him and asked him to devote himself to illustrate my quarterly. He was supposed just then to be dying [Beardsley was a consumptive]; and as I entered the room, and saw him lying on a couch horribly white, I wondered if I had come too late. He was full of ideas, full of enthusiasm, and I think it was then that he suggested the name *SAVOY*,

[1] *The Aesthetic Adventure* (1945)
[2] *The Romantic '90's* by Richard Le Gallienne (1926)
[3] *Aubrey Beardsley* by Arthur Symons (1898)

finally adopted after endless changes and uncertainties.'[1]

Beardsley is known best, of course, for the sinister rococo of his drawings. Art fanciers in their multitudes have been fascinated by his tall voluptuous women 'always with great clouds of black hair and faces slightly ugly',[2] while 'spiders, curtains, tassels and lanterns'[3] crowded out every available inch in the background of corners of his compositions. But Beardsley also had ambitions to write, and contributed three poems and an unfinished romance to *The Savoy*. Understandably, these literary productions have been over-shadowed by his draughtmanship, though they contain a distinction all their own.

Symons believed that Beardsley would rather have been a great writer than a great artist. 'I remember', he writes, 'on one occasion, when he had to fill up a form of admission to some library to which I was introducing him, his insistence on describing himself as "man of letters". At one time he was going to write an essay on *Les Liaisions Dangereuses*, at another he had planned a book on Rousseau. But his plans for writing changed even more quickly than his plans for doing drawings, and with less profitable results in the meantime . . . Here, too, he was terribly anxious to excel.'[4]

There is an astonishing similarity between his unfinished literary fantasy and his prolific drawings. The same principle of close-set design, of intricate inlay work, distinguishes them both. As Roger Fry observed in 1904, 'Beardsley had . . . in an extraordinary degree, the decorative impulse, the motive which made the mediaeval scribe flourish his pen all over the margins of his vellum page; and spurred by this impulse, he had the patience of an Indian craftsman, covering whole sheets with minute dots and scarcely perceptible lines.'[5] This describes admirably the creative principle at work in such drawings as 'The

[1] Ibid.
[2] *Opening Day* by David Gascoyne (1933)
[3] Ibid.
[4] *Aubrey Beardsley*
[5] 'Aubrey Beardsley' (*Vision and Design*)

Toilet'[1] and 'The Baron's Prayer'[2] (from *The Rape of the Lock* illustrations) or 'The Mysterious Rose Garden'[3] and the style of writing in *Under the Hill.* Here is the young Abbé Fanfreluche:

> His hand, slim and gracious as La Marquise du Deffand's in the drawing by Carmontelle, played nervously about the gold hair that fell upon his shoulders like a finely curled peruke, and from point to point of a precise toilet the fingers wandered, quelling the little mutinies of cravat or ruffle.[4]

In prose this intagliated manner of writing diminished the tempo of exposition: the narrative is hidden behind the description. Strangely enough, his verse escapes the bad effects of excessive cataloguing. There is, in fact, a directness about it rare in the poetry of the 'nineties. His least successful piece *The Ballad of a Barber*[5] gets off to an effective quick start:

> Here is the tale of Carrousel,
> The barber of Meridian Street,
> He cut, and coiffed, and shaved so well,
> That all the world was at his feet.

This has a traditional economy of statement which late-nineteenth-century verse often lacked. The poem is also possessed of a wit which no 'nineties poet, save Plarr perhaps, can equal:

> Such was his art he could with ease
> Curl wit into the dullest face
>
> He felt as foolish as a fable,
> And feeble as a pointless jest.

Arthur Symons, generally so discerning, apparently

[1], [2], and [3] *Aubrey Beardsley* by Arthur Symons
[4] *Under the Hill* (*The Savoy*)
[5] *The Savoy*, No. 3 (July 1896)

thought poorly of the poem; and certainly, by implication, underrated that brilliant piece *The Three Musicians*. 'We spent', he recalls, 'two whole days on the grassy ramparts of the old castle at Arques-la-Bataille, near Dieppe; I working at something or other in one part, he working at *The Three Musicians* in another. The eight stanzas of that amusing piece of verse are really, in their own way, a *tour de force*; by sheer power of will, by deliberately saying to himself, "I will write a poem," and by working with such strenuous application that at last a certain result, the kind of result he had willed, did really come about, he succeeded in doing what he had certainly no natural aptitude for doing.'[1]

The best words on Beardsley as a poet have been written by Osbert Burdett. ' "The Ballad of a Barber" and "The Three Musicians" ', he declared, 'pick up the eighteenth century tradition at the point where it was dropped by Pope, and the later poem especially recreates this tradition in terms of our own day. . . . They were, no doubt experiments, but the literary precocity that they show is so astonishing that we would willingly exchange for them a whole library of more pretentious verse. . . . The two shorter pieces [*The Three Musicians* and the translation from Catullus] deserve a place in any late Victorian anthology.'[2] The version from Catullus he praises highly too, rating it as Beardsley's best piece of verse. 'I do not think', he writes, 'that any competent critic will deny the lines beginning

By ways remote and distant waters sped

are a beautiful poem . . . the result is a genuine poem, not an artificial piece of verse-making, for the lines move us by a dirge-like chant full of the pagan wistfulness which provoked them.'[3]

It is very possible that, had he lived, Beardsley would

[1] *Aubrey Beardsley* by Arthur Symons
[2] *The Beardsley Period*
[3] Ibid.

have added new dimensions to both his visual and literary expression. The letters he wrote to his publisher Smithers when he was often staining 'many a fair handkerchief red with blood',[1] are full of gaiety and vitality, and when other men would have written with lack of spirit, self-pityingly, he is full of his own irrepressible jokes. 'The little creature handing hats', he tells his correspondent in answer to a query, 'is not an infant but an unstrangled abortion.'[2]

It was the same gamin spirit of mischief which had led him earlier, as art editor of *The Yellow Book*, to play up his careful publisher. 'Poor Lane', as Le Gallienne records, 'had a rather nerve-wracking time with Beardsley, who, for the fun of it, was always trying to slip some indecency into his covers, not apparent without close scrutiny . . . It was quite a game of hide-and-seek . . . in which Beardsley took a boyish delight.'[3]

And with the very last letters of all—those written on the brink of his death-bed—a new seriousness enters in. 'Heine', he notes in one of them, 'certainly cuts a poor figure beside Pascal. If Heine is the great warning, Pascal is the great example to all artists and thinkers. He understood that to become a Christian the man of letters must sacrifice his gifts just as Magdalen must sacrifice her beauty.'[4] Three weeks before his death he remarks: 'I have been reading a good deal of S. Alphonsius Liguori; no one dispels depression more than he. Reading his loving exclamations, so lovingly reiterated, it is impossible to remain dull and sullen.'[5] Certain of the later drawings point to the fuller horizon 'which he was created to scan'.[6] Both as to design and emotional tone 'Et in Arcadia Ego' has a gravity of feeling absent before.[7]

Beardsley was received into the Roman Catholic Church in 1897 and died at Mentone on 16th March 1898.

[1] *Letters from Aubrey Beardsley to Leonard Smithers* (1937)
[2] Ibid.
[3] Ibid.
[4] *The Last Letters of Aubrey Beardsley* (1915)
[5] Ibid.
[6] Father John Gray's Introduction to *The Last Letters of Aubrey Beardsley*
[7] *Aubrey Beardsley* by Arthur Symons

The Three Musicians

Along the path that skirts the wood,
The three musicians wend their way,
Pleased with their thoughts, each other's mood,
Franz Himmel's latest roundelay,
The morning's work, a new-found theme, their breakfast
and the summer day.

One's a soprano, lightly frocked
In cool white muslin that just shows
Her brown silk stockings gaily clocked,
Plump arms and elbows tipped with rose,
And frills of petticoats and things, and outlines as the
warm wind blows.

Beside her a slim, gracious boy
Hastens to mend her tresses' fall,
And dies her favour to enjoy,
And dies for *reclame* and recall
At Paris and St Petersburgh, Vienna and St James's
Hall.

The third's a Polish Pianist
With big engagements everywhere,
A light heart and an iron wrist.
And shocks and shoals of yellow hair,
And fingers that can trill on sixths and fill beginners
with despair.

The three musicians stroll along
And pluck the ears of ripened corn,
Break into odds and ends of song,
And mock the woods with Siegfried's horn,
And fill the air with Gluck, and fill the tweeded tourist's soul with scorn.

The Polish genius lags behind,
And, with some poppies in his hand,
Picks out the strings and wood and wind
Of an imaginary band,
Enchanted that for once his men obey his beat and understand.

The charming cantatrice reclines
And rests a moment where she sees
Her château's roof that hotly shines
Amid the dusky summer trees,
And fans herself, half shuts her eyes, and smoothes the frock about her knees.

The gracious boy is at her feet,
And weighs his courage with his chance;
His fears soon melt in noonday heat.
The tourist gives a furious glance,
Red as his guide-book grows, moves on, and offers up a prayer for France.

The Ballad of a Barber

Here is the tale of Carrousel,
The barber of Meridian Street,
He cut, and coiffed, and shaved so well,
That all the world was at his feet.

The King, the Queen, and all the Court,
To no one else would trust their hair,
And reigning belles of every sort
Owed their successes to his care.

With carriage and with cabriolet
Daily Meridian Street was blocked,
Like bees about a bright bouquet
The beaux about his doorway flocked.

Such was his art he could with ease
Curl wit into the dullest face;
Or to a goddess of old Greece
Add a new wonder and a grace.

All powders, paints, and subtle dyes,
And costliest scents that men distill,
And rare pomades, forgot their price
And marvelled at his splendid skill.

The curling irons in his hand
Almost grew quick enough to speak,
The razor was a magic wand
That understood the softest cheek.

Yet with no pride his heart was moved;
He was so modest in his ways!
His dainty task was all he loved,
And now and then a little praise.

An equal care he would bestow
On problems simple or complex;
And nobody had seen him show
A preference for either sex.

How came it then one sunny day,
Coiffing the daughter of the King,
He lengthened out the least delay
And loitered in his hairdressing?

The Princess was a pretty child,
Thirteen years old, or thereabout.
She was as joyous and as wild
As spring flowers when the sun is out.

Her gold hair fell down to her feet
And hung about her pretty eyes;
She was as lyrical and sweet
As one of Schubert's melodies.

Three times the barber curled a lock,
And thrice he straightened it again;
And twice the irons scorched her frock,
And twice he stumbled in her train.

His fingers lost their cunning quite,
His ivory combs obeyed no more;
Something or other dimmed his sight,
And moved mysteriously the floor.

He leant upon the toilet table,
His fingers fumbled in his breast;
He felt as foolish as a fable,
And feeble as a pointless jest.

He snatched a bottle of Cologne,
And broke the neck between his hands;
He felt as if he was alone,
And mighty as a king's commands.

The Princess gave a little scream,
Carrousel's cut was sharp and deep;
He left her softly as a dream
That leaves a sleeper to his sleep.

He left the room on pointed feet;
Smiling that things had gone so well.
They hanged him in Meridian Street.
You pray in vain for Carrousel.

Catullus

Carmen CI

By ways remote and distant waters sped,
Brother, to thy sad grave-side am I come,
That I may give the last gifts to the dead,
And vainly parley with thine ashes dumb:
Since she who now bestows and now denies
Hath ta'en thee, hapless brother, from mine eyes.

But lo! these gifts, the heirlooms of past years,
Are made sad things to grace thy coffin shell,
Take them, all drenchèd with a brother's tears,
And, brother, for all time, hail and farewell!

Ernest Dowson

1867–1900

ERNEST CHRISTOPHER DOWSON was born at The Grove, Belmont Hill, Lee, Kent, on 2nd August 1867, the son of an East End dry-dock owner.

His life has been fully chronicled by the American scholar Mark Longaker who has also edited his stories and poems;[1] but two diverse trends of appreciation make it difficult for the reader to interpret his life aright. The first of these—the bohemian—is best represented by Arthur Symons, who wrote a memoir[2] of the poet on his death, later affixed to the editions of his poems. The second—the respectable or discreet—is represented by his friend Victor Plarr, a worthy and charming man, who decided to restore Dowson's credit. 'There were', he wrote, 'certainly two Dowsons—one the vexed and torn spirit of the biographers . . . the other a Dowson *intime*, known, I venture to think, to very few, but by those few greatly loved.'[3]

Symons has been attacked for the 'synthetic Bohemianism'[4] of his account, and some of his facts are certainly

[1] *Ernest Dowson* by Mark Longaker (1944)
The Stories of Ernest Dowson, ed. by Mark Longaker (1947)
The Poems of Ernest Dowson, ed. by Mark Longaker (1962)
[2] 'Ernest Dowson' (*Studies in Prose and Verse*) (1904)
[3] *Ernest Dowson, Reminiscences 1887–1898* (1914)
[4] *The Poetical Works of Dowson*, ed. with an Introduction by Desmond Flower (1934)

misleading; but the white-washing process, commenced by Plarr, cannot be too indefinitely extended. The following amusing incident, recorded by Yeats, is a case in point.

The trouble had started with some words written by Symons in his magazine *The Savoy*.[1] Ostensibly on a book of Dowson's poems, Symons' causerie was largely occupied with painting the poet as a vagabond figure. 'He will not mind', wrote Symons, with clearly no sense of what his words suggested, 'if I speak of him with some of that frankness which we usually reserve for the dead.' But best of all was Symons' conclusion: 'And now, indifferent to most things, in the shipwrecked quietude of a sort of self-exile, he is living, I believe, on a remote foreign sea-coast.' Dowson, who—as Symons knew—was never farther off than Brittany, was naturally annoyed at this picture, and wrote to Symons protesting against it. He was, he said, living quietly and with model industry in a little country village. But before Dowson's letter arrived, his correspondent, Yeats recalled, 'received a wire, "arrested, sell watch and send proceeds." Dowson's watch had been left in London—and then another wire, "Am free." Dowson, or so ran the tale . . . had got drunk and fought the baker, and a deputation of villagers had gone to the magistrate and pointed out that Monsieur Dowson was one of the most illustrious of English poets. "Quite right to remind me," said the magistrate, "I will imprison the baker." '[2] There are certain apochryphal touches here; but there clearly were 'two Dowsons', as much in the flesh as in print. Yeats remembers that the poet who possessed 'so much dignity and reserve' needed to be lectured by his friend Lionel Johnson 'out of the Fathers upon chastity'. Johnson, slyly continues Yeats, 'boasted of the great good done thereby. But the rest of us counted the glasses emptied in their talk.'[3] As he observes else-

[1] 'A Literary Causerie: On a Book of Verses' (*The Savoy*, No. 4) (August 1896)

[2] 'The Tragic Generation' (*The Trembling of the Veil*)

[3] Ibid.

where: 'Johnson and Dowson, friends of my youth, were dissipated men, the one a drunkard, the other a drunkard and mad about women.'[1]

As to appearance, Le Gallienne remembers him as 'a frail appealing figure, with an almost painfully sensitive face, delicate as a silver point, recalling at once Shelley and Keats, too worn for one so young'.[2] Wilde found him 'persistently and perversely wonderful',[3] and Yeats 'gentle, affectionate, drifting',[4] while Plarr was never tired of insisting on his courteous manners.[5]

Yet despite his vices, his frustration, his sickness, Dowson produced a sizeable body of work. His first book *Dilemmas: Stories and Studies in Sentiment* was published by John Lane in 1895. Dowson then changed his publisher, and in 1896 Leonard Smithers brought out his *Verses* ('printed on Japanese vellum and bound in parchment, with a cover design in gold by Aubrey Beardsley'[6]) to be followed the next year by *The Pierrot of the Minute*. As well as contributing new stories to *The Savoy*, he engaged in much translation work, into English from the French for Smithers and others: Arouet de Voltaire's *La Pucelle The Maid of Orleans*, Choderlos de la Clos' *Dangerous Acquaintances*, Richard Muther's *The History of Modern Painting*, and fiction by Balzac and Zola. His last volume of verse, including five prose poems, was published in 1899 under the title of *Decorations*. Desmond Flower's edition of Dowson prints forty unpublished or uncollected poems, making, all told, 114 lyrical pieces.

He also wrote two novels in collaboration with Arthur Moore, a friend of his Queen's College, Oxford, days: *A Comedy of Masks* (1893) and *Adrian Rome* (1899). It is amusing to reflect that Dowson cared more for his prose than for his verse, though—as Symons correctly pro-

[1] 'Per amica silentia Lunae' (*Mythologies*) (1959)
[2] *The Romantic '90's*
[3] To Ernest Dowson, ? 16th June 1897 (*Letters of Oscar Wilde*)
[4] 'The Tragic Generation' (*The Trembling of the Veil*)
[5] *Ernest Dowson: Reminiscences 1887–1897*
[6] *The Men of the Nineties* by Bernard Muddiman (1920)

phesied—'it is not by his prose that he will live, exquisite as that prose was at its best'.[1]

Twentieth-century critical opinion differs widely on the value of his work. Desmond Flower, on the strength of his eight poems in the sequence *Of a little girl*, claims him as a 'master of the sonnet'.[2] Professor Grierson allows him 'unmistakable lyrical inspiration',[3] while Professor Ifor Evans sees him as 'the poet symbolic of the eighteen-nineties . . . in verse what Beardsley was in pictorial art'.[4] Kenneth Hopkins in his *English Poetry: A Short History* speaks of how Dowson's poem *Cynara* gives him his title as laureate of the decade, and Symons calls the same poem 'one of the greatest lyrical poems of our time', a lyric 'in which he epitomized himself and his whole life'.[5] Patric Dickinson has choicely praised the classical purity of Dowson's dictum comparing his archetype line

Wine and woman and song

with Symons'

Wine and women and cigars

to the great disadvantage of the second, whose vulgarity becomes apparent.[6]

On the other hand, Herbert Palmer, in his *Post Victorian Poetry* urges that 'the technical excellence of Dowson's few exceedingly good poems . . . must not blind us to his lack of technical achievement in general', while John Heath-Stubbs in *The Darkling Plain* (1900) speaking of the 'Rhymer' poets, allows him this meagre praise: 'Within the narrow limits in which these poets chose to work, Dowson comes nearest to success—but that is not very near. He survives in a shadowy way, through the charm of, at most, two or three minor poems.' But it is R. L. Mègroz,

[1] 'Ernest Dowson' (*Studies in Prose and Verse*)
[2] *The Poetical Works of Dowson* (1934)
[3] *Lyrical Poetry from Blake to Hardy* (1928)
[4] *English Poetry in the Later Nineteenth Century* (1933)
[5] 'Ernest Dowson' (*Studies in Prose and Verse*)
[6] *Here and Now:* an anthology ed. by Sylvia Read (1943)

who has attacked his reputation most fiercely in his book *Modern English Poetry, 1882–1932* (1933). Dowson, he holds, 'has left scarcely anything which would not be adequately described by the title of "Decorations" '. He compares Dowson's poem *To a Dead Child* with Robert Bridges' poem with a similar title. 'The difference', he writes, 'is not merely that Bridges' poem happens to be one of his best, which Dowson's is not. There is the difference in the quality of mind and the expression of feeling . . . There was nothing in Dowson to be called up except a sigh of self-pity.'

When Dowson died in the house of his friend and biographer Robert Sherard at Catford on 23rd February 1900,[1] Wilde wrote to Leonard Smithers, publisher of them both: 'I am greatly distressed to hear of Ernest's death . . . Poor wounded wonderful fellow that he was, a tragic reproduction of all tragic poetry. I hope bay-leaves will be laid on his tomb, and rue, and myrtle too, for he knew what love is.'[2] He was buried in the Roman Catholic part of Lewisham Cemetery ('Laus Deo!'[3] Lionel Johnson had written to Le Gallienne on the poet's conversion a few years previously).

There is a fictional portrait of Dowson in Marian Plarr's novel *Cynara* (1933) where he is featured as the character Ernest.

[1] A full account of Dowson's death is given by Sherard in his book *Twenty-five Years in Paris* (1905)

[2] *The Letters of Oscar Wilde*

[3] *The Romantic '90's*

Villanelle of the Poet's Road

Wine and woman and song,
  Three things garnish our way:
Yet is day over long.

Lest we do our youth wrong,
  Gather them while we may:
Wine and woman and song.

Three things render us strong,
  Vine leaves, kisses and bay;
Yet is day over long.

Unto us they belong,
  Us the bitter and gay,
Wine and woman and song.

We, as we pass along,
  Are sad that they will not stay;
Yet is day over long.

Fruits and flowers among,
  What is better than they:
Wine and woman and song;
  Yet is day over long.

NON SUM QUALIS ERAM BONAE SUB REGNO CYNARAE

Last night, ah, yesternight, betwixt her lips and mine
There fell thy shadow, Cynara! thy breath was shed
Upon my soul between the kisses and the wine;
And I was desolate and sick of an old passion,
  Yea, I was desolate and bowed my head:
I have been faithful to thee, Cynara! in my fashion.

All night upon mine heart I felt her warm heart beat,
Night-long within mine arms in love and sleep she lay;
Surely the kisses of her bought red mouth were sweet;
But I was desolate and sick of an old passion,
  When I awoke and found the dawn was gray:
I have been faithful to thee, Cynara! in my fashion.

I have forgot much, Cynara! gone with the wind,
Flung roses, roses riotously with the throng,
Dancing to put thy pale lost lilies out of mind;
But I was desolate and sick of an old passion,
  Yea, all the time, because the dance was long:
I have been faithful to thee, Cynara! in my fashion.

I cried for madder music and for stronger wine,
But when the feast is finished and the lamps expire,
Then falls thy shadow, Cynara! the night is thine;
And I am desolate and sick of an old passion,
  Yea, hungry for the lips of my desire:
I have been faithful to thee, Cynara! in my fashion.

ERNEST DOWSON

O MORS! QUAM AMARA EST MEMORIA TUA HOMINI PACEM HABENTI IN SUBSTANTIIS SUIS

Exceeding sorrow
  Consumeth my sad heart!
Because to-morrow
  We must depart,
Now is exceeding sorrow
  All my part!

Give over playing,
  Cast thy viol away:
Merely laying
  Thine head my way:
Prithee, give over playing,
  Grave or gay.

Be no word spoken;
  Weep nothing: let a pale
Silence, unbroken
  Silence prevail!
Prithee, be no word spoken,
  Lest I fail!

Forget to-morrow!
  Weep nothing: only lay
In silent sorrow
  Thine head my way:
Let us forget to-morrow,
  This one day!

DUM NOS FATA SINUNT, OCULOS SATIEMUS AMORE—Propertius

Cease smiling, Dear! a little while be sad,
  Here in the silence, under the wan moon;
Sweet are thine eyes, but how can I be glad,
  Knowing they change so soon?

For Love's sake, Dear, be silent! Cover me
  In the deep darkness of thy falling hair:
Fear is upon me and the memory
  Of what is all men's share.

O could this moment be perpetuate!
  Must we grow old, and leaden-eyed and gray,
And taste no more the wild and passionate
  Love sorrows of to-day?

Grown old, and faded, Sweet! and past desire,
  Let memory die, lest there be too much ruth,
Remembering the old, extinguish fire
  Of our divine, lost youth.

O red pomegranate of thy perfect mouth!
  My lips' life-fruitage, might I taste and die
Here in thy garden, where the scented south
  Wind chastens agony;

Reap death from thy live lips in one long kiss,
  And look my last into thine eyes and rest:
What sweets had life to me sweeter than this
  Swift dying on thy breast?

Or, if that may not be, for Love's sake, Dear!
  Keep silence still, and dream that we shall lie,
Red mouth to mouth, entwined, and always hear
  The south wind's melody.

Here in thy garden, through the sighing boughs,
  Beyond the reach of time and chance and change,
And bitter life and death, and broken vows,
  That sadden and estrange.

AH, DANS CES MORNES SÉJOURS LES JAMAIS SONT LES TOUJOURS

—Paul Verlaine

You would have understood me, had you waited;
  I could have loved you, dear! as well as he:
Had we not been impatient, dear! and fated
  Always to disagree.

What is the use of speech? Silence were fitter:
  Lest we should still be wishing things unsaid.
Though all the words we ever spake were bitter,
  Shall I reproach you dead?

Nay, let this earth, your portion, likewise cover
  All the old anger, setting us apart:
Always, in all, in truth was I your lover;
  Always, I held your heart.

I have met other women who were tender,
  As you were cold, dear! with a grace as rare.
Think you, I turned to them, or made surrender
  I who had found you fair?

Had we been patient, dear! ah, had you waited,
  I had fought death for you, better than he:
But from the very first, dear! we were fated
  Always to disagree.

Late, late, I come to you, now death discloses
  Love that in life was not to be our part:
On your low lying mound between the roses,
  Sadly I cast my heart.

I would not waken you: nay! this is fitter;
  Death and the darkness give you unto me;
Here we who loved so, were so cold and bitter,
  Hardly can disagree.

Spleen

I was not sorrowful, I could not weep,
And all my memories were put to sleep.

I watched the river grow more white and strange,
All day till evening I watched it change.

All day till evening I watched the rain
Beat wearily upon the window pane.

I was not sorrowful, but only tired
Of everything that ever I desired.

Her lips, her eyes, all day became to me
The shadow of a shadow utterly.

All day mine hunger for her heart became
Oblivion, until the evening came,

And left me sorrowful, inclined to weep,
With all my memories that could not sleep.

To One in Bedlam

With delicate, mad hands, behind his sordid bars,
Surely he hath his posies, which they tear and twine;
Those scentless wisps of straw, that miserable line
His strait, caged universe, whereat the dull world stares.

Pedant and pitiful. O, how his rapt gaze wars
With their stupidity! Know they what dreams divine
Lift his long, laughing reveries like enchanted wine,
And make his melancholy germane to the stars?

O lamentable brother! if those pity thee,
Am I not fain of all thy lone eyes promise me;
Half a fool's kingdom, far from men who sow and reap,
All their days, vanity? Better than mortal flowers,
Thy moon-kissed roses seem: better than love or sleep,
The star-crowned solitude of thine oblivious hours!

ERNEST DOWSON

Extreme Unction

Upon the eyes, the lips, the feet,
  On all the passages of sense,
The atoning oil is spread with sweet
  Renewal of lost innocence.

The feet, that lately ran so fast
  To meet desire, are soothly sealed;
The eyes, that were so often cast
  On vanity, are touched and healed.

From troublous sights and sounds set free;
  In such a twilight hour of breath,
Shall one retrace his life, or see,
  Through shadows, the true face of death?

Vials of mercy! Sacring oils!
  I know not where or when I come,
Nor through what wanderings and toils,
  To crave of you Viaticum.

Yet when the walls of flesh grow weak,
  In such an hour, it well may be,
Through mist and darkness, light will break,
  And each anointed sense will see.

Vesperal

Strange grows the river on the sunless evenings!
The river comforts me, grown spectral, vague and dumb:
Long was the day; at last the consoling shadows come:
Sufficient for the day are the day's evil things!

Labour and longing and despair the long day brings;
Patient till evening men watch the sun go west;
Deferred, expected night at last brings sleep and rest:
Sufficient for the day are the day's evil things!

At last the tranquil Angelus of evening rings
Night's curtain down for comfort and oblivion
Of all the vanities observed by the sun:
Sufficient for the day are the day's evil things!

So, some time, when the last of all our evenings
Crowneth memorially the last of all our days,
Not loth to take his poppies man goes down and says,
'Sufficient for the day were the day's evil things!'

Villanelle of Marguerites

'A little, *passionately, not at all?*'
She casts the snowy petals on the air:
And what care we how many petals fall!

Nay, wherefore seek the seasons to forestall?
It is but playing, and she will not care,
A little, passionately, not at all!

She would not answer us if we should call
Across the years: her visions are too fair;
And what care we how many petals fall!

She knows us not, nor recks if she enthrall
With voice and eyes and fashion of her hair,
A little, passionately, not at all!

Knee-deep she goes in meadow grasses tall,
Kissed by the daisies that her fingers tear:
And what care we how many petals fall!

We pass and go: but she shall not recall
What men we were, nor all she made us bear:
'A little, passionately, not at all!'
And what care we how many petals fall!

The Three Witches

All the moon-shed nights are over,
  And the days of gray and dun;
There is neither may nor clover,
  And the day and night are one.

Not an hamlet, not a city
  Meets our strained and tearless eyes;
In the plain without a pity,
  Where the wan grass droops and dies.

We shall wander through the meaning
  Of a day and see no light,
For our lichened arms are leaning
  On the ends of endless night.

We, the children of Astarte,
  Dear abortions of the moon,
In a gay and silent party,
  We are riding to you soon.

Burning ramparts, ever burning!
  To the flame which never dies
We are yearning, yearning, yearning,
  With our gay and tearless eyes.

In the plain without a pity,
  (Not an hamlet, not a city)
  Where the wan grass droops and dies.

Carthusians

Through what long heaviness, assayed in what strange
 fire,
 Have these white monks been brought into the way of
 peace,
Despising the world's wisdom and the world's desire,
 Which from the body of this death bring no release?

Within their austere walls no voices penetrate;
 A sacred silence only, as of death, obtains;
Nothing finds entry here of loud or passionate;
 This quiet is the exceeding profit of their pains.

From many lands they came, in divers fiery ways;
 Each knew at last the vanity of earthly joys;
And one was crowned with thorns, and one was crowned
 with bays,
 And each was tired at last of the world's foolish noise.

It was not theirs with Dominic to preach God's holy
 wrath,
 They were too stern to bear sweet Francis' gentle
 sway;
Theirs was a higher calling and a steeper path,
 To dwell alone with Christ, to meditate and pray.

A cloistered company, they are companionless,
 None knoweth here the secret of his brother's heart:
They are but come together for more loneliness,
 Whose bond is solitude and silence all their part.

O beatific life! Who is there shall gainsay,
  Your great refusal's victory, your little loss,
Deserting vanity for the more perfect way,
  The sweeter service of the most dolorous Cross.

Ye shall prevail at last! Surely ye shall prevail!
  Your silence and austerity shall win at last:
Desire and mirth, the world's ephemeral lights shall fail,
  The sweet star of your queen is never overcast.

We fling up flowers and laugh, we laugh across the
    wine;
  With wine we dull our souls and careful strains of art;
Our cups are polished skulls round which the roses
    twine:
  None dares to look at Death who leers and lurks
    apart.

Move on, white company, whom that has not sufficed!
  Our viols cease, our wine is death, our roses fail:
Pray for our heedlessness, O dwellers with the Christ!
  Though the world fall apart, surely ye shall prevail.

To a Lady Asking Foolish Questions

Why am I sorry, Chloe? Because the moon is far:
And who am I to be straitened in a little earthly star?

Because thy face is fair? And what if it had not been,
The fairest face of all is the face I have not seen.

Because the land is cold, and however I scheme and plot,
I cannot find a ferry to the land where I am not.

Because thy lips are red and thy breasts upbraid the
  snow?
(There is neither white nor red in the pleasance where
  I go.)

Because thy lips grow pale and thy breasts grow dun and
  fall?
I go where the wind blows, Chloe, and am not sorry at
  all.

Ad Manus Puellae

I was always a lover of ladies' hands!
Or ever mine heart came here to tryst,
For the sake of your carved white hands' commands;
The tapering fingers, the dainty wrist.
The hands of a girl were what I kissed.

I remember an hand like a *fleur-de-lys*
When it slid from its silken sheath, her glove;
With its odours passing ambergris:
And that was the empty husk of love.
Oh, how shall I kiss your hands enough?

They are pale with the pallor of ivories;
But they blush to the tips like a curled sea-shell:
What treasure, in kingly treasuries,
Of gold and spice for the thurible,
Is sweet as her hands to hoard and tell?

I know not the way from your finger tips,
Nor how I shall gain the higher lands,
The citadel of your sacred lips:
I am captive still of my pleasant bands,
The hands of a girl, and most of your hands.

On the Birth of a Friend's Child

Mark the day white, on which the Fates have smiled:
Eugenio and Egeria have a child.
On whom abundant grace kind Jove imparts
If she but copy either parent's parts.
Then, Muses! long devoted to her race,
Grant her Egeria's virtues and her face;
Nor stop your bounty there, but add to it
Eugenio's learning and Eugenio's wit.

To William Theodore Peters on his Renaissance Cloak

The cherry-coloured velvet of your cloak
  Time hath not soiled: its fair embroideries
Gleam as when centuries ago they spoke
  To what bright gallant of Her Daintiness,
  Whose slender fingers, long since dust and dead,
  For love or courtesy embroidered
The cherry-coloured velvet of this cloak.

Ah! cunning flowers of silk and silver thread,
  That mock mortality? the broidering dame,
The page they decked, the kings and courts are dead:
  Gone the age beautiful; Lorenzo's name,
  The Borgia's pride are but an empty sound;
  But lustrous still upon their velvet ground,
Time spares these flowers of silk and silver thread.

Gone is that age of pageant and of pride:
  Yet don your cloak, and haply it shall seem,
The curtain of old time is set aside;
  As through the sadder coloured throng you gleam;
  The glamour and the grace of yesterday:
The elder, brighter age of pomp and pride.

Benedicto Domini

Without the sullen noises of the street!
  The voice of London, inarticulate,
Hoarse and blaspheming, surges in to meet
  The silent blessing of the Immaculate.

Dark is the church, and dim the worshippers,
  Hushed with bowed heads as though by some old
    spell,
While through the incense-laden air there stirs
  The admonition of a silver bell.

Dark is the church, save where the altar stands,
  Dressed like a bride, illustrious with light,
Where one old priest exalts with tremulous hands
  The one true solace of man's fallen plight.

Strange silence here: without, the sounding street
  Heralds the world's swift passage to the fire:
O Benediction, perfect and complete!
  When shall men cease to suffer and desire?

ERNEST DOWSON

A Requiem

Neobule, being tired,
Far too tired to laugh or weep,
From the hours, rosy and gray,
Hid her golden face away.
Neobule, fain of sleep,
Slept at last as she desired!

Neobule! is it well,
That you haunt the hollow lands,
Where the poor, dead people stray,
Ghostly, pitiful and gray,
Plucking, with their spectral hands,
Scentless blooms of asphodel?

Neobule, tired of death
Of the flowers that I threw
On her flower-like, fair feet,
Sighed for blossoms not so sweet,
Lunar roses pale and blue,
Lilies of the world beneath.

Neobule! ah, too tired
Of the dreams and days above!
Where the poor, dead people stray,
Ghostly, pitiful and gray
Out of life and out of love,
Sleeps the sleep which she desired.

After Paul Verlaine

The sky is up above the roof
  So blue, so soft!
A tree there, up above the roof,
  Swayeth aloft.

A bell within that sky we see,
  Chimes low and faint:
A bird upon that tree we see,
  Maketh complaint.

Dear God! is not the life up there,
  Simple and sweet?
How peacefully are borne up there
  Sounds of the street!

What hast thou done, who comest here,
  To weep alway?
Where hast thou laid, who comest here,
  Thy youth away?

After Paul Verlaine

COLLOQUE SENTIMENTAL

Into the lonely park all frozen fast,
A while ago there were two forms who passed.

Lo, are their lips fallen and their eyes dead,
Hardly shall a man hear the words they said.

Into the lonely park, all frozen fast,
There came two shadows who recall the past.

'Dost thou remember our old ecstasy?'—
'Wherefore should I possess that memory?'—

'Doth thine heart beat at my sole name alway?
Still dost thou see my soul in visions?' 'Nay!'—

'They were fair days of joy unspeakable,
Whereon our lips were joined?'—'I cannot tell.'—

'Were not the heavens blue, was not hope high?'—
'Hope has fled vanquished down the darkling sky.'—

So through the barren oats they wandered,
And the night only heard the words they said.

After Paul Verlaine

IL PLEUT DOUCEMENT SUR LA VILLE
—RIMBAUD

Tears fall within mine heart,
As rain upon the town:
Whence does this languor start,
Possessing all mine heart?

O sweet fall of the rain
Upon the earth and roofs!
Unto an heart in pain,
O music of the rain!

Tears that have no reason
Fall in my sorry heart:
What! there was no treason?
This grief hath no reason.

Nay! the more desolate,
Because, I know not why,
(Neither for love nor hate)
Mine heart is desolate.

After Paul Verlaine

SPLEEN

Around were all the roses red,
The ivy all around was black.

Dear, so thou only move thine head,
Shall all mine old despairs awake!

Too blue, too tender was the sky,
The air too soft, too green the sea.

Always I fear, I know not why,
Some lamentable flight from thee.

I am so tired of holly-sprays
And weary of the bright box-tree,

Of all the endless, country ways;
Of everything alas! save thee.

The Moon Maiden's Song

from *The Pierrot of the Minute*

Sleep! Cast thy canopy
  Over this sleeper's brain;
Dim grow his memory,
  When he awake again.

Love stays a summer night,
  Till lights of morning come;
Then takes her wingèd flight
  Back to her starry home.

Sleep! Yet thy days are mine;
  Love's seal is over thee:
Far though my ways from thine,
  Dim though thy memory.

Love stays a summer night,
  Till lights of morning come;
Then takes her wingèd flight
  Back to her starry home.

Epigram

Because I am idolatrous and have besought,
With grievous supplication and consuming prayer,
The admirable image that my dreams have wrought
Out of her swan's neck and her dark, abundant hair:
The jealous gods who brook no worship save their own,
Turned my live idol marble and her heart to stone.

Beyond

Love's aftermath! I think the time is now
That we must gather in, alone, apart
The saddest crop of all the crops that grow,
  Love's aftermath.
Ah, sweet,—sweet yesterday, the tears that start
Can not put back the dial; this is, I trow,
Our harvesting! Thy kisses chill my heart,
Our lips are cold; averted eyes avow
The twilight of poor love: we can but part,
Dumbly and sadly, reaping as we sow,
  Love's aftermath.

A Valediction

If we must part,
Then let it be like this;
Not heart on heart,
Nor with the useless anguish of a kiss;
But touch mine hand and say:
'Until to-morrow or some other day,
If we must part.'

Words are so weak
When love hath been so strong:
Let silence speak:
'Life is a little while, and love is long;
A time to sow and reap,
And after harvest a long time to sleep,
But words are weak.'

VITAE SUMMA BREVIS SPEM NOS VETAT INCOHARE LONGAM

They are not long, the weeping and the laughter,
Love and desire and hate
I think they have no portion in us after
We pass the gate.

They are not long, the days of wine and roses:
Out of a misty dream
Our path emerges for a while, then closes
Within a dream.

Victor Plarr

1863–1929

VICTOR GUSTAVE PLARR, son of a Doctor of Science from Alsace, was born near Strassburg on 21st June 1863. His mother was British, the daughter of a Lombard Street banker; and it is probably from her that he inherited his poetic temperament since she both wrote and published verse.

The boy came to Scotland at the age of seven, his father's house having been burnt down in the Franco-Prussian War. He was educated at the Madras College, St Andrews, at Tonbridge School, and at Worcester College, Oxford, where he read Modern History and took a second-class honours degree. At Oxford he met Ernest Dowson; and his chief claim to recognition is the record he left of this friendship, *Ernest Dowson: Reminiscences 1887–1897* (1914), a book of great charm written in a faultless prose of quiet distinction. On its publication, Selwyn Image—Slade Professor of Fine Arts (1908–14) and companion of the Rhymers Club days—wrote to Plarr: 'It is a most exquisite piece of work, a real tribute to our dear dead Friend such as would have been after his own delicate heart.'[1] The book is full of fascinating sidelights on the men of the time, marred—if one may speak so harshly—only by its author's sense of honour and discretion.

[1] 7th January 1915. *Selwyn Image: Letters*, ed. A.H. Mackmurdo (1932)

On coming down from Oxford, he obtained the post of Librarian at King's College, London, later becoming Librarian to the Royal College of Surgeons in 1897.

Plarr was a member of the Rhymers Club and contributed to both its anthologies (1892 and 1894) and also to *The Garland* (1898). Before the publication of his first volume of verse *In the Dorian Mood* (1896), Lionel Johnson in some notes to his friend Katherine Tynan, was judiciously singing his praises. 'You might mention Dowson and Victor Plarr', he wrote, 'as men sure to be successful when their first books appear . . . Plarr is delightful, a kind of half-French, half-Celtic Dobson with nature and the past and dying traditions and wild races for his theme.'[1]

Plarr is, indeed, delightful, though largely on account of a couple of lyrics—the witty *Epitaphium Citharistriae* and the formally skilful *Ad Cinerarium*, a piece of succinct perfection such as Gautier might have envied. These are two of the choicest poems written during the 'nineties.

Culturally, Plarr was a literary conservative: today he would be called reactionary. What he says of the little town Thegnhurst, just outside London, in his story *Miss Peele's Apotheosis: A Study of Extrasuburban Amenities*,[2] may well be applied to himself: 'Thegnhurst is unimpeachably genteel—using the term in all good faith . . . The snobbishness of Thegnhurst is of a shade so subtle that it is difficult to apprehend it with the naked eye of criticism—it exists, but so mingled with better things, with honest pride in honourable tradition, that the man who in conversation tries to surprise it is often fain to give up the attempt with a blush and the sense of having said something stupidly ill-bred.' Like Thegnhurst, Plarr hated 'vulgarity and eccentricity . . . Brummagen sectarianism . . . faddist politics . . . scepticism . . . the Bohemianism of the arts . . . 'appy 'Amstead on a Sunday'.[3]

[1] *Literary Essays of Ezra Pound* (1954)
[2] *Pageant* (1897)
[3] Ibid.

Perhaps, however, for all his disclaimers, one should not evoke an image of the man as too relentlessly *de rigeur*. Morley Roberts, the novelist, who remembers him as 'the mildest but soundest minded' of all the Rhymer poets, recalls one afternoon spent in their company when Lionel Johnson got drunk three times with absinthe but which he admitted was 'a literary Bohemian success'. 'So successful was it,' continues Roberts, 'that when we broke up Plarr and Dowson, both smoking cigarettes, embraced on the landing and then fell downstairs, emitting sparks like a Catherine wheel.'[1]

Plarr's output was not great. He edited the fifteenth edition of *Men and Women of the Time: A Dictionary of Contemporaries* (1899), in which he inserted the lives and careers of a number of his friends. In 1903 he published *Literary Etiquette*, its title proclaiming the purist that Plarr was. This was followed by *The Tragedy of Asgard* (1905). He also made a number of translations from French and Greek.

Plarr, who once described his recreations as 'sleep and pastel drawing', lived at Wimbledon, where he died on 28th January 1929.

Ezra Pound has featured him as 'Monsieur Verog' in his poem *Hugh Selwyn Mauberley: Life and Contacts*.

[1] *Post-Victorian Poetry* by Herbert Palmer (1939)

Epitaphium Citharistriae

Stand not uttering sedately
  Trite oblivious praise above her!
Rather say you saw her lately
  Lightly kissing her last lover.

Whisper not, 'There is a reason
  Why we bring her no white blossom':
Since the snowy bloom's in season
  Stow it on her sleeping bosom:

Oh, for it would be a pity
  To o'erpraise her or to flout her:
She was wild, and sweet, and witty—
  Let's not say dull things about her.

Ad Cinerarium

Who in this small urn reposes,
  Celt or Roman, man or woman,
Steel of steel, or rose of roses?

Whose is the dust set rustling slightly,
  In its hiding-place abiding,
When this urn is lifted lightly?

Sure some mourner deemed immortal
  What thou holdest and enfoldest,
Little house without a portal!

When the artificers had slowly
  Formed thee, turned thee, sealed thee,
    burned thee,
Freighted with thy freightage holy,

Sure he thought there's no forgetting
  All the sweetness and completeness
Of his rising, of her setting,

And so bade them grave no token,
  Generation, age, or nation,
On thy round side still unbroken;—

Let them score no cypress verses,
  Funeral glories, prayers, or stories,
Mourner's tears, or mourner's curses,

Round thy brown rim time hath polished,—
Let thee dumbly cold and comely
As some shrine of gods abolished.

Ah, 'twas well! It scarcely matters
What is sleeping in the keeping
Of this house of human tatters,—

Steel of steel, or rose of roses,
Man, or woman, Celt or Roman,
If but soundly he reposes!

Arthur Symons

1865–1945

ARTHUR WILLIAM SYMONS was born at Milford Haven on 21st February 1865 at 11 p.m. Yeats' uncle, George Pollexfen, with whom the two poets once went to stay, cast Symons' horoscope for him. According to it, he was 'serious, thoughtful, reserved, a good student'. He had 'intense intuition . . . a highly strung sensitive nature'. Persons born at the hour of his birth were said to be 'very imaginative subjects, to see visions, dream dreams and to be, for the most part, believers in the unseen world'. Most of this fits Symons well, and he kept its four written pages all his life.

He was the son of a Cornish Methodist minister. In the 'nineties there was a conscious revival of all things Celtic, and Symons always stressed this element in his make-up. 'Bone by bone, blood by blood, I am a Cornishman' he wrote in *Jezebel Mort*, his last book of verse.

A freely imaginative account of his early years 'A Prelude to Life'[1] shows a boy at school, full of the same patchy brilliance as characterized the young Lionel Johnson: 'I was never able to go in for matriculation . . . because, while I could have come out easily at the top in most of the subjects, there were always one or two in which I could do nothing.' He had, however, a flair for

[1] 'A Prelude to Life' (*Spiritual Adventures*) (1905)

languages, teaching himself to read in these tongues by following passages in them as the Bible was read out in chapel.

Precociousness and isolation characterised his life with his family. 'We were surrounded', he confessed, 'by commonplace, middle-class people, and I hated commonplace and the middle-classes.'[1] His escape out of this was into music and literature. At fifteen he was writing to an ex-teacher and friend, 'You will be interested to know that I am learning Chopin's Funeral March—a glorious piece!'[2] and all his life he remained an ardent pianist.

Nineteen years later he paid a personal homage to the work of the same composer:

> O passionate music pallid with ghostly fears,
> Chill with the coming of rain, the beginning of tears,
> I come to you, fleeing you, finding you, fever of
> love![3]

As a critic he was to speak often on this subject, his chief essays in this field being found in *Plays, Acting & Music* (1903), and *Studies in Seven Arts* (1906).

Scholarship and criticism provided a further outlet, and by the time he was twenty-one he had edited certain plays of Shakespeare and other Elizabethan dramatists, as well as having written a book on Browning which obtained a favourable review from Walter Pater.

By twenty he was modelling his style on Pater. 'What Browning was to me in verse, Pater from about the age of seventeen had been to me in prose. It was from reading Pater's studies in the *History of the Renaissance*, that I first realised that prose could be a fine art.'[4] The arch-hierophant of the aesthetic movement, Pater was named as the *dedicé* of Symons' first volume of verse *Days and Nights* (1889), to which he accorded a sympathetic notice.

[1] Ibid.
[2] *Arthur Symons: A Critical Biography* by Roger Lhombreaud (1963)
[3] 'Chopin' (*Images of Good and Evil*) (1899)
[4] *A Study of Walter Pater* (1932)

'In this new poet,' he wrote, 'the rich poetic vintage of our time has run clear at last.'[1]

Most of these poems were lurid enough; but they did contain a certain dramatic power, a certain determined modernity, as well as examples of that synaesthesia—that combining and transferring of sense impressions—which marks much symbolist poetry. *The Opium Smoker* demonstrates this well:

> I am engulfed, and drown deliciously.
> Soft music like a perfume, and sweet light
> Golden with audible odours exquisite,
> Swathes me with cerements for eternity.[2]

The book contained seven translations, six from French poetry. This bespoke a cardinal affinity in Symons. In 1890 he met Verlaine in Paris, and in 1893 the French poet came to visit him in the Temple at Fountain Court where he was then living. Symons translated many of Verlaine's poems[3] and the pieces in his volume *Silhouettes* (1892) have the same sketchy but neat impressionism which we find in Verlaine's *Aquarelles*.

> The grey and misty night,
> Slim trees that hold the night among
> Their branches, and, along
> The vague Embankment, light on light.[4]

Symons now consciously embraced Verlaine's technique of handling words, which he described in the following impressionistic terms: 'They transform themselves for him into music, colour, and shadow; a disembodied music, diaphanous colours, luminous shadows . . .'[5]

Along with Verlaine, Symons was also translating Mallarmé whom he had met in Paris at the poet's famous Tuesday soirées. In an article on *The Decadent Movement*

[1] 'A Poet with Something to say' (*Pall Mall Gazette*) (23rd March 1889)
[2] *Days and Nights*
[3] *The Knave of Hearts* (1913)
[4] 'In the Temple' (*Silhouettes*)
[5] 'Paul Verlaine' (*Symbolist Movement in Literature*) (1899)

ERNEST DOWSON

ARTHUR SYMONS

in Literature[1] he attempted to establish a parallel between symbolism and impressionism or, as we might say, between Mallarmé and Verlaine. 'Impressionism and symbolism', he wrote, 'are really working on the same hypothesis, applied in different directions . . . The Impressionist . . . would flash upon you in a new, sudden way so exact an image of what you have just seen . . . The Symbolist in this new, sudden way, would flash upon you the "soul" of that which can be apprehended only by the soul—the finer sense of things unseen, the deeper meaning of things evident.'

Up to 1896, it is the impressionist interest and technique which dominates Symons' poems. *London Nights* (1895), dedicated to Paul Verlaine, is a verse-kaleidoscope of the music-hall, of which he was an enthusiastic patron as well as being ballet critic for *The Star*. He sought, as he said, to make a Degas out of 'happy accidents . . . momentary points of view . . . [and] chance felicities of light and shade and movement'.[2] *London Nights* is full of such a backstage poetry:

> The shadows of the gaslit wings,
> Come softly crawling down our way;
> Before the curtain someone sings,
> The music comes from far away;
> I stand beside you in the wings . . .[3]

Impressionism is an art of appearances, an art of superficies; not an art in depth. The 'deeper meaning' which Symbolism seeks was not to be found in Symons' poetry until he had been deeply hurt by experience.

His earlier verses are full of 'light loves' and the 'chance romances of the street'.

> The little bedroom papered red,
> The gas's faint malodorous light,
> And one beside me in the bed,
> Who chatters, chatters, half the night.[4]

[1] *Harpers* (November 1893)
[2] *Cities and Sea-coasts and Islands* (1919)
[3] 'At the Foresters' [4] 'Leves Amores' (*London Nights*)

Since 1893, Symons had known a nineteen-year-old girl of the chorus at the Empire. This was Lydia, or Bianca (as she appeared in *London Nights*). In his private papers,[1] Symons has recorded the terrible hold this young woman had upon him. They broke finally in 1895, and Symons left England for two months, to find distraction and rest at Dieppe where he busied himself with preparing the first number of *The Savoy* in company with its art editor Aubrey Beardsley.

Symons has left an *imaginative* account of this relationship in his volume of poems *Amoris Victima* (1897). They are sensational and melodramatic though that is no reason for doubting the *human* sincerity behind them. What is more important than the direct transcription of most of this experience is the general deepening of his mind as a result of this loss and sorrow.

The new note is to be heard both in his verse and prose. *The Symbolist Movement in Literature*, published in the last year of the decade and dedicated to his friend Yeats, proclaims that truth is with the mystic. A literature of 'smiling and many-coloured appearances'[2] no longer satisfies him. 'All we have to ask of death is the meaning of life, and we are waiting all through life to ask that question.'[3] Not that Symbolism provides the answer. 'The final uncertainty remains, but we can seem to knock less helplessly at closed doors, coming so much closer to the once terrifying eternity of things about us, as we come to look upon these things as shadows, through which we have our shadowy passage.'[4]

The *Epilogue* to his volume of verse *Images of Good and Evil*, appearing the same year, conveys the new deeper note: 'O little waking hour of life out of sleep!' The best of Symons' poetry now gains an added dimension by becoming, for the first time, properly conscious of mortality.

Along with Mallarmé and the French symbolists, his verse began to show the influence of those writers associ-

[1] *Arthur Symons: A Critical Biography* by Roger Lhombreaud
[2],[3], and [4] *The Symbolist Movement in Literature*

ated with the 'Celtic Twilight'. The first of these, of course, was Yeats who had shared chambers with him in Fountain Court in the earlier years of the decade. Yeats has spoken of 'an Irish poet whose rhythms are like the cry of a seabird in autumn twilight',[1] and some of Symons' pieces in *Images of Good and Evil* have the same weary plaintiveness in their music:

> I heard the sighing of the reeds
> In the grey pool in the green land,
> The sea-wind in the long reeds sighing
> Between the green hills and the sand.[2]

'I see', write Yeats, in 1897, 'in the arts of every country these faint lights and faint colours and faint outlines and faint energies which many call "the decadence", and which I, because I believe that the arts lie dreaming of things to come, prefer to call the autumn of the body.'[3] Such an atmosphere of enervation curiously bordering on apprehension informs these later poems of Symons, and is especially to be found in his masterly translations from Mallarmé: *Sigh*, *Sea-wind*, *Anguish*, and *Herodiade*.

Symons' work, in verse and prose, extends beyond the nineteenth century. It is, however, renewed by few ideas after 1900. In 1901 he was married; and in 1908, in Italy, he experienced a complete nervous breakdown. He was certified mentally insane, but discharged in 1910, living after that date, for the most part, quietly in his cottage at Wittersham in Kent, and dying on 22nd January 1945.

Such attention as Symons has received of late years has chiefly been paid to his criticism. In 1957, Dame Edith Sitwell spoke of him as a 'great critic of the 1890's and 1900's now most unwisely neglected'.[4] For Iain Fletcher, writing in 1953, he was 'a good minor poet, an excellent translator, a major critic'.[5] Frank Kermode, discussing the

[1] 'The Autumn of the Body' (*Essays and Introductions*) (1961)
[2] *By the Pool of the Third Rosses*
[3] 'The Autumn of the Body' (*Essays and Introductions*)
[4] *The Sunday Times* (5th May 1957)
[5] *The Complete Poems of Lionel Johnson*

twentieth century's adaptation of the ideas of symbolism, finds Symons and his work 'crucial'. 'He knew', maintains Kermode, 'how to synthesise the earlier English tradition —particularly Blake . . . with Pater and those European symbolists he knew so well. Symons also had a considerable part in the associated revival of interest in Donne and the Jacobean poets',[1] who were later to influence Eliot.

An American critic, Wilbur Marshall Urban, described him as 'a perfect instrument for impressionism'.[2] Against this must be set the severe assessment of his contemporary, Lionel Johnson. 'Symons', he wrote to his friend Katherine Tynan, 'is a slave to impressionism, whether the impression be precious or not. A London fog, the blurred, tawny lamplights, the red omnibus, the dreary rain, the depressing mud, the glaring gin-shop, the slatternly shivering women: three dexterous stanzas telling you that and nothing more.'

There is an impishly belittling vignette of Symons in a broadcast article by Max Beerbohm included in John Morris' collection *From the Third Programme: A Ten-Years' Anthology*, 1956. The most sympathetic account of Symons by those who knew him personally is to be found in Yeats' *Autobiographies*. 'Symons,' he wrote, 'more than any other man I have ever known, could slip as it were into the mind of another.' It was no doubt this quality which made him a receptive critic.

[1] *Romantic Image* (1957)
[2] *The Atlantic Monthly* (1914)

Intermezzo

TO THE MEMORY OF CHARLES BAUDELAIRE

Nini Patte-en-l'Air

(*Casino de Paris*)

The gold Casino's Spring parterre
Flowers with the Spring, this golden week;
Glady, Toloche, Valtesse, are there;
But all eyes turn as one to seek
The drawers of Nini Patte-en-l'air.

Surprising, sunset-coloured lace,
In billowy clouds of gold and red,
They whirl and flash before one's face;
The little heel above her head
Points an ironical grimace.

And mark the experimental eyes,
The naughty eloquence of feet,
The appeal of subtly quivering thighs,
The insinuations indiscreet
Of pirouetting draperies.

What exquisite indecency,
Select, supreme, severe, an art!
The art of knowing how to be
Part lewd, aesthetical in part,
And *fin-de-siècle* essentially.

The Maenad of the Decadence,
Collectedly extravagant,
Her learned fury wakes the sense
That, fainting, needs for excitant
This science of concupiscence.

(Paris, May 14, 1892)

Palm Sunday: Naples

Because it is the day of Palms,
Carry a palm for me,
Carry a palm in Santa Chiara,
And I will watch the sea;
There are no palms in Santa Chiara
To-day or any day for me.

I sit and watch the little sail
Lean side-ways on the sea,
The sea is blue from here to Sorrento
And the sea-wind comes to me,
And I see the white clouds lift from Sorrento
And the dark sail lean upon the sea.

I have grown tired of all these things,
And what is left for me?
I have no place in Santa Chiara,
There is no peace upon the sea;
But carry a palm in Santa Chiara,
Carry a palm for me.

ARTHUR SYMONS

Intermezzo: Venetian Nights

II. AT THE DOGANA

Night, and the silence of the night,
In Venice; far away, a song;
As if the lyric water made
Itself a serenade;
As if the water's silence were a song
Sent up into the night.

Night, a more perfect day,
A day of shadows luminous,
Water and sky at one, at one with us;
As if the very peace of night,
The older peace than heaven or light,
Came down into the day.

Stella Maris

Why is it I remember yet
You, of all women one has met,
In random wayfare, as one meets
The chance romances of the streets,
The Juliet of a night? I know
Your heart holds many a Romeo.
And I, who call to mind your face
In so serene a pausing-place,
Where the pure bright expanse of sea,
The shadowy shore's austerity,

Seem a reproach to you and me,
I too have sought on many a breast
The ecstasy of love's unrest,
I too have had my dreams, and met
(Ah me!) how many a Juliet.
Why is it, then, that I recall
You, neither first nor last of all?
For, surely as I see to-night
The phantom of the lighthouse light,
Against the sky across the bay,
Fade, and return, and fade away,
So surely do I see your eyes
Out of the empty night arise;
Child, you arise and smile to me
Out of the night, out of the sea,
The Nereid of a moment there,
And is it sea-weed in your hair?
O lost and wrecked, how long ago,
Out of the drowning past, I know
You come to call me, come to claim
My share of your delicious shame.
Child, I remember, and can tell
One night we loved each other well,
And one night's love, at least or most
Is not so small a thing to boast.
You were adorable, and I
Adored you to infinity,
The nuptial night too briefly borne
To the oblivion of morn.
Ah! no oblivion, for I feel
Your lips deliriously steal
Along my neck, and fasten there;
I feel the perfume of your hair,
I feel your breast that heaves and dips
Desiring my desirous lips,
And that ineffable delight
When souls turn bodies, and unite

In the intolerable, the whole
Rapture of the embodied soul.
That joy was ours, we passed it by;
You have forgotten me, and I
Remember you thus, strangely won
An instant from oblivion.
And, I, remembering, would declare
That joy, not shame is ours to shame,
Joy that we had the frank delight
To choose the chances of one night,
Out of vague nights, and days at strife,
So infinitely full of life.
What shall it profit me to know
Your heart holds many a Romeo?
Why should I grieve, though I forget
How many another Juliet?
Let us be glad to have forgot
That roses fade, and loves are not,
As dreams immortal, though they seem
Almost as real as a dream.
It is for this I see you rise,
A wraith, with starlight in your eyes,
Where calm hours weave, for such a mood
Solitude out of solitude;
For this, for this, you come to me
Out of the night, out of the sea.

Perfume

Shake out your hair about me, so,
That I may feel the stir and scent
Of those vague odours come and go
The way our kisses went.

Night gave this priceless hour of love,
But now the dawn steals in apace,
And amorously bends above
The wonder of your face.

'Farewell' between our kisses creeps,
You fade, a ghost, upon the air;
Yet ah! the vacant place still keeps
The odour of your hair.

At Dieppe

RAIN ON THE DOWN

Night, and the down by the sea,
And the veil of rain on the down;
And she came through the mist and the rain to me
From the safe warm lights of the town.

The rain shone in her hair,
And her face gleamed in the rain;
And only the night and the rain were there
And she came to me out of the rain.

At Dieppe

AFTER SUNSET

The sea lies quieted beneath
The after-sunset flush
That leaves upon the heaped grey clouds
The grape's faint purple blush.

Pale, from a little space in heaven
Of delicate ivory,
The sickle moon and one gold star
Look down upon the sea.

At Dieppe

ON THE BEACH

Night, a grey sky, a ghostly sea,
The soft beginning of the rain;
Black on the horizon, sails that wane
Into the distance mistily.

The tide is rising, I can hear
The soft roar broadening far along;
It cries and murmurs in my ear
A sleepy old forgotten song.

Softly the stealthy night descends,
The black sails fade into the sky:
Is not this, where the sea-line ends,
The shore-line of infinity?

I cannot think or dream; the grey
Unending waste of sea and night,
Dull, impotently infinite,
Blots out the very hope of day.

Quest

I chase a shadow through the night,
A shadow unavailingly;
Out of the dark, into the light,
I follow, follow: is it she?

Against the wall of sea outlined,
Outlined against the windows lit,
The shadow flickers, and behind
I follow, follow after it.

The shadow leads me through the night
To the grey margin of the sea;
Out of the dark, into the light,
I follow unavailingly.

White Heliotrope

The feverish room and that white bed,
The tumbled skirts upon a chair,
The novel flung half-open where
Hat, hair-pins, puffs, and paints, are spread;

The mirror that has sucked your face
Into its secret deep of deeps,
And there mysteriously keeps
Forgotten memories of grace;

And you, half dressed and half awake,
Your slant eyes strangely watching me,
And I, who watch you drowsily,
With eyes that, having slept not, ache;

This (need one dread? nay, dare one hope?)
Will rise, a ghost of memory, if
Ever again my handkerchief
Is scented with White Heliotrope.

April Midnight

Side by side through the streets at midnight,
Roaming together,
Through the tumultuous night of London,
In the miraculous April weather.

Roaming together under the gaslight,
Day's work over,
How the Spring calls to us, here in the city
Calls to the heart from the heart of a lover!

Cool the wind blows, fresh in our faces,
Cleansing, entrancing,
After the heat and the fumes and the footlights,
Where you dance and I watch your dancing.

Good it is to be here together,
Good to be roaming,
Even in London, even at midnight,
Lover-like in a lover's gloaming.

You the dancer and I the dreamer,
Children together,
Wandering lost in the night of London,
In the miraculous April weather.

City Nights

IN THE TEMPLE

The grey and misty night,
Slim trees that hold the night among
Their branches, and, along
The vague Embankment, light on light.

The sudden, racing lights!
I can just hear, distinct, aloof,
The gaily clattering hoof
Beating the rhythm of festive nights.

The gardens to the weeping moon
Sigh back the breath of tears.
O the refrain of years on years
'Neath the weeping moon!

In Fountain Court

The fountain murmuring of sleep,
A drowsy tune;
The flickering green of leaves that keep
The light of June;
Peace, through a slumbering afternoon,
The peace of June.

A waiting ghost, in the blue sky,
The white curved moon;
June, hushed and breathless, waits, and I
Wait too, with June;
Come, through the lingering afternoon,
Soon, love, come soon.

For a Picture of Watteau

Here the vague winds have rest;
The forest breathes in sleep,
Lifting a quiet breast;
It is the hour of rest.

How summer glides away!
An autumn pallor blooms
Upon the cheek of day.
Come, lovers, come away!

But here, where dead leaves fall
Upon the grass, what strains,
Languidly musical,
Mournfully rise and fall?

Light loves that woke with spring
This autumn afternoon
Beholds meandering,
Still, to the strains of spring.

Your dancing feet are faint,
Lovers: the air recedes
Into a sighing plaint,
Faint, as your loves are faint.

It is the end, the end,
The dance of love's decease.
Feign no more now, fair friend!
It is the end, the end.

Clair De Lune

In the moonlight room your face,
Moonlight-coloured, fainting white
And the silence of the place
Round about us in the night,
And my arms are round about you
In the silence of the night.

Lips that are not mine to kiss,
Lips how often kissed in vain,
Broken seal of memories,
Where the kisses come again
That the lips of all your lovers
Laid upon your lips in vain;

Eyes that are not mine to keep
In the mirror of my eyes,
Where I tremble lest from sleep
Other ghosts should re-arise;
Why enthrall me with your magic,
Haunting lips, triumphant eyes?

For the silence of the night
Swims around me like a stream,
And your eyes have caught the light
Of a moon-enchanted dream,
And your arms glide round about me,
And I fade into a dream.

(IN IRELAND)

By the Pool at the Third Rosses

I heard the sighing of the reeds
In the grey pool in the green land,
The sea-wind in the long reeds sighing
Between the green hill and the sand.

I heard the sighing of the reeds
Day after day, night after night;
I heard the whirring wild ducks flying,
I saw the sea-gulls' wheeling flight.

I heard the sighing of the reeds
Night after night, day after day,
And I forgot old age, and dying,
And youth that loves. and love's decay.

I heard the sighing of the reeds
At noontide and at evening,
And some old dream I had forgotten
I seemed to be remembering.

I heard the sighing of the reeds;
Is it in vain, is it in vain
That some old peace I had forgotten
Is crying to come back again?

ARTHUR SYMONS

(FROM SAN JUAN DE LA CRUZ)

The Obscure Night of the Soul

Upon an obscure night,
Fevered with love in love's anxiety,
(O hapless-happy plight!)
I went, none seeing me,
Forth from my house where all things quiet be.

By night, secure from sight,
And by the secret stair, disguisedly,
(O hapless-happy plight!)
By night, and privily,
Forth from my house where all things quiet be.

Blest night of wandering,
In secret, where by none might I be spied,
Nor I see anything;
Without a light or guide,
Save that which in my heart burnt in my side.

That light did lead me on,
More surely than the shining of noontide,
Where well I knew that one
Did for my coming bide;
Where he abode might none but he abide.

O night that didst lead thus,
O night more lovely than the dawn of light,
O night that broughtest us,
Lover to lover's sight,
Lover with loved in marriage of delight!

Upon my flowery breast,
Wholly for him, and save himself for none,
There did I give sweet rest
To my beloved one;
The fanning of the cedars breathed thereon.

When the first moving air
Blew from the tower, and waved his locks aside.
His hand, with gentle care,
Did wound me in the side,
And in my body all my senses died.

All things I then forgot,
My cheek on him who for my coming came;
All ceased, and I was not,
Leaving my cares and shame
Among the lilies, and forgetting them.

From Santa Teresa

Let mine eyes see thee,
Sweet Jesus of Nazareth
Let mine eyes see thee,
And then see death.

Let them see that care
Roses and jessamine;
Seeing thy face most fair
All blossoms are therein.
Flower of seraphin,
Sweet Jesus of Nazareth,
Let mine eyes see thee,
And then see death.

Nothing I require
Where my Jesus is;
Anguish all desire,
Saving only this;
All my help is his,
He only succoureth.
Let mine eyes see thee,
Sweet Jesus of Nazareth,
Let mine eyes see thee,
And then see dcath.

(FROM STÉPHANE MALLARMÉ)

Sea-Wind

The flesh is sad, alas! and all the books are read.
Flight, only flight! I feel that birds are wild to tread
The floor of unknown foam, and to attain the skies!
Nought, neither ancient gardens mirrored in the eyes,
Shall hold this heart that bathes in waters its delight,
O nights! nor yet my waking lamp, whose lonely light
Shadows the vacant paper, whiteness profits best,
Nor the young wife who rocks her baby on her breast.
I will depart! O steamer, swaying rope and spar,
Lift anchor for exotic lands that lie afar!
A weariness, outworn by cruel hopes, still clings
To the last farewell handkerchief's last beckonings!
And are not these, the masts inviting storms, not these
That an awakening wind bends over wrecking seas,
Lost, not a sail, a sail, a flowering isle, ere long?
But, O my heart, hear thou, hear thou the sailors' song!

(FROM STÉPHANE MALLARMÉ)

Sigh

My soul, calm sister, towards thy brow, whereon scarce grieves
An autumn strewn already with its russet leaves,
And towards the wandering sky of thine angelic eyes,
Mounts, as in melancholy gardens may arise
Some faithful fountain sighing whitely towards the blue!
Towards the blue pale and pure that sad October knew,
When, in those depths, it mirrored languors infinite,
And agonising leaves upon the waters white,
Windily, drifting, traced a furrow cold and dun,
Where, in one long last ray, lingered the yellow sun:

(FROM PAUL VERLAINE: FÊTES GALANTES)

Mandoline

The singers of serenades
Whisper their fated vows
Unto fair listening maids
Under the singing boughs.

Tircis, Aminte, are there,
Clitandre has waited long,
And Damis for many a fair
Tyrant makes many a song.

Their short vests, silken and bright,
Their long pale silken trains,
Their elegance of delight,
Twine soft blue silken chains.

And the mandolines and they,
Faintlier breathing, swoon
Into the rose and grey
Ecstasy of the moon.

(FROM PAUL VERLAINE: FÊTES GALANTES)

Les Indolents

Bah! spite of Fate, that says us nay,
Suppose we die together, eh?
—A rare conclusion you discover!

—What's rare is good. Let us die so,
Like lovers in Boccaccio.
—Ha! ha! ha! you fantastic lover!

—Nay, not fantastic. If you will,
Fond, surely irreproachable.
Suppose, then, that we die together?

—Good sir, your jests are fitlier told
Than when you speak of love or gold.
Why speak at all, in this glad weather?

Whereat, behold them once again,
Tircis beside his Dorimène,
Not far from two blithe rustic rovers,

For some caprice of idle breath
Deferring a delicious death.
Ha! ha! ha! what fantastic lovers!

(FROM THÉOPHILE GAUTIER)

Posthumous Coquetry

Let there be laid, when I am dead,
Ere 'neath the coffin lid I lie,
Upon my cheek a little red,
A little black about the eye.

For I in my close bier would fain,
As on the night his vows were made,
Rose-red eternally remain,
With khol beneath my blue eye laid.

Wind me no shroud of linen down
My body to my feet, but fold
The white folds of my muslin gown
With thirteen flounces, as of old.

This shall go with me where I go:
I wore it when I won his heart;
His first look hallowed it, and so,
For him, I laid the gown apart.

No immortelles, no broidered grace
Of tears upon my cushion be;
Lay me on my own pillow's lace,
My hair across it, like a sea.

John Davidson

1857-1909

JOHN DAVIDSON was born in Barrhead, Renfrewshire, on 11th April 1857. Among the poets of the 'nineties he was something of an anomaly. Into the English gentility, the Irish charm, and Welsh fire of the Rhymers, he brought an irreverent and disputative vigour. His early years had been full of hardship, and he looked upon certain poets of this group—the products of leisure and privilege—with a mixture of jealousy and contempt. He had, too, a forceful intellect; and was not inclined to sit silent and impressed at the smooth southern ritual of Art for Art's sake. The exclusive constrained aestheticism of the meetings at 'The Cheshire Cheese' exasperated him. 'Once when I had praised Herbert Horne [a member of the Rhymers] for his knowledge and his taste,' Yeats tells us, 'he burst out, "If a man must be a connoisseur, let him be a connoisseur in women." '[1] The limited fund of ideas, making up the common mental kitty of the Rhymers, provoked Davidson as they did Yeats. Strangely, the two men could not abide each other.

The events of his life have been well related by Maurice Lindsay in his Introduction to a choice of Davidson's verse.[2] His father was a minister of the Evangelical Union,

[1] 'The Tragic Generation' (*The Trembling of the Veil*)
[2] *John Davidson: A Selection of his Poems* (1961)

whose doctrines were not of too illiberal an order. Throughout his existence, however, Davidson rebelled against Christianity and the father-figure. Like Symons, he appeared to love his mother, while feeling aversion for his other parent. His accusation breaks out in the poem he wrote when he was forty:

Think, mother, think!
Look back upon your fifty wretched years
And show me anywhere the hand of God.
Your husband saving souls—O paltry souls
That need salvation! lost the grips of things,
And left you penniless with none to aid
But me the prodigal.[1]

While other members of the Rhymers, placed in more fortunate circumstances, were growing up slowly according to some settled pattern of 'the English gentleman', Davidson found himself pitchforked out of school at the age of thirteen to work in the chemical laboratory of a sugar refinery. Between 1870 and 1889, he was mostly employed as a teacher, though he managed to secure for himself a year as arts student at Edinburgh University.

In later years he described the Philistinism in which he was brought up, a cultural claustrophobia 'which is both the nitrogen and oxygen of Greenock',[2] his home town. Escapism by way of verse suggested itself as the not unusual life-line—but what to do with the poetry when written? Davidson's lack of *savoir faire* surpassed that of most young men, for at twenty-one he wrote to Swinburne—whom he had once met in Glasgow—enclosing some poems and asking that his senior should try to get them published if he found them to have merit. The letter—addressed to 'The Nightingale of Poets' 'with every good wish from a singing bird of some description, and probably quality'—went, as did the following one, unanswered. Davidson, though disappointed, was undaunted. He had always a

[1] 'A Woman and her Son' (*New Ballads*) (1897)
[2] *John Davidson: A Selection of his Poems*

good opinion of himself, which later, under pressure of bitterness, was to become megalomania. 'If I am what I take myself to be,' he wrote to Swinburne in his young man's letter, 'my opinion carries great weight.'

Before he came to London in 1889, to follow his friend Professor John Nichol southwards to a writing career, he had published locally and at Glasgow four books, including *Scaramouch in Naxos* (1889), a curious pantomime-drama, later to be illustrated by Beardsley. The 'Prologue' to the play, spoken by Silenus, describes the spirit of pantomime as 'a good-natured nightmare . . . frivolity whipping its schoolmaster, common sense'. But this old conventional idea of the medium seemed inadequate to the author, and Silenus reports him as saying that 'Pantomime seems to be the best hope [for a development in drama]. It contains in crude forms, humour, poetry and romance. It is childhood of a new poetical comedy.'

In achievement, *Scaramouch in Naxos* is not all that impressive. But it does possess a whimsical humour—many *fin-de-siècle* poets were rather over-earnest—and shows its author's determination to open up his medium and 'make it new'. 'Here we have Davidson', comments Holbrook Jackson, 'as early as 1888, concerned about something . . . elastic enough to contain a big expression of modernity.'[1] Davidson's concern with pantomime may perhaps suggest to us T.S. Eliot's interest in the music-hall[2] and the early fruit of this in *Sweeney Agonistes*.

Davidson's early years in London, as far as sales go, were a success. He boasted to Yeats that his agent got him forty pounds a ballad and that his last book of verse (*Ballads and Songs*, 1894) had made him £300. His relation to the Decadent movement was always accidental. 'He was', declares Holbrook Jackson, 'as strange to the Rhymers Club as he was to the Fabian Society or the Humanitarian League, and although circumstances brought him into The Bodley Head group of writers, giving some

[1] *The Eighteen Nineties* (1913)
[2] 'The Possibility of a Poetic Drama' (*The Sacred Wood*)[2] (1920)

of his books decorations by Beardsley, and his portrait by Will Rothenstein to *The Yellow Book*, the facts must be set down to Mr John Lane's sense of what was new and strong in literature rather than to any feeling of kinship on Davidson's part.'[1] The novel which he published in 1895—*A Full and True Account of the Wonderful Mission of Earl Lavender*—is one of those anti-movement fictions, such as Robert Hichens' *The Green Carnation* or G. S. Street's *The Autobiography of a Boy* in which the affectation of decadence is mocked. As he wrote in a poetical note to the book:

> Oh! our age and style perplexes
> All our Elders time has famed;
> On our sleeves we wear our sexes,
> Our diseases, unashamed.

The first volume of his poems to be published in London proudly carried a 'period' title *In a Music Hall* (1891). In the same year he joined the Rhymers Club, but did not contribute to either of its anthologies. In fact, he was soon in hot-water with its milder, more decorous members, whom he described as lacking in 'blood and guts'. He had, indeed, attempted to remedy the low metabolism of the group by the addition of four Scotsmen. 'He brought all four', reports Yeats, 'upon the same evening, and one read out a poem upon the Life Boat, evidently intended for a recitation; another described how, when gold-digging in Australia, he had fought and knocked down another miner for doubting the rotundity of the earth; while of the remainder I can remember nothing except that they excelled in argument. He insisted upon their immediate election, and the Rhymers, through that complacency of good manners whereby educated Englishmen so often surprise me, obeyed, though secretly resolved never to meet again; and it cost me seven hours' work to get another meeting, and vote the Scotsmen out.'[2]

It is clear that Davidson affected different people

[1] *The Eighteen Nineties* by Holbrook Jackson
[2] 'The Tragic Generation' (*The Trembling of the Veil*)

differently. Edgar Jepson, in his *Memories of a Victorian*, remembered him 'in his short beard, silk hat and morning coat' as resembling 'a commercial traveller at loggerheads with the world'. On Frank Harris, writing in *Contemporary Portraits*, he left the following impression: 'He was a little below middle height, but strongly built with square shoulders and remarkably fine face and head: the features were almost classically regular, the eyes dark brown and large, the forehead high, the hair and moustache black. [Actually he wore a *toupée* which successfully took in the artist Will Rothenstein, who was sketching a likeness of his head, till Max Beerbohm pointed out its existence.] His manners were perfectly frank and natural: he met everyone in the same unaffected kindly human way: I never saw a trace in him of snobbishness or incivility.' Possibly it was Richard Le Gallienne who came nearest to a just objectivity when he balanced the pros and cons of Davidson 'whose personality was rocky and stubborn and full of Scotch fight, with no little of Scotch pig-headedness. But with him, as with the lion in Holy Writ, within whose jaws the wild bees built their honeycomb, it was a case of *ex forte dulcedo*: for beneath his proud, rather pragmatic exterior, his nature was full of human kindness and repressed tenderness.'[1]

Davidson's boom on the poetry market was unfortunately short-lived. Not so long after his first boasting to Yeats on the size of his literary income, he told him: 'The fires are out . . . and I must hammer the cold iron.'[2]

But failure and disappointment only confirmed Davidson the more in a sense of his own rightness. His embattled atheism became more proclamatory, and to this inflammable he added the explosive of Nietzsche's philosophy, currently translated into English by a fellow Scot, Thomas Common. Nietzsche, at his best, has elegance and poise; but these were qualities which evaded Davidson, who from his reading only increased his own stock of aggressiveness.

[1] *The Romantic 90's* (1926)
[2] 'The Tragic Generation' (*The Trembling of the Veil*)

By 1907, his verse had degenerated into this kind of ranting:

> And the long gestant Teuton vengeance, cognate
> With puberty of soul that swells our thought,
> Dethrones the decadent neo-Hebraism
> Which Christianity is, and with its new
> Cosmogony of uncreated worlds
> Begins to shape a non-creating God.
>
> (*The Triumph of Mammon*)

And with unsuccess and a flaunting philosophy, his megalomaniac tendencies increased. The year in which the above lines were published, Neil Munro called on the poet at Streatham as emissary of the Greenock Burns Club. The welcome he got was far from warm. Keeping him upon the doorstep, Davidson lectured him on his lack of respect. 'You should have thought,' he told Munro. 'You should have said (this with finger tapping forehead and eyes fixed on some far horizon), here is a man different from other men! I must not treat him like other men! I must not go knocking at his door and expect to be received. I must write to ask if he will receive me.'[1]

Another two years of struggle, aided by too small a Civil List pension, brought him to breaking-point. On the last day of his life he wrote the Preface to his final book of poems and posted his manuscript to his publishers from Penzance where he was holidaying with his family. Grant Richards, opening the parcel, found the following note: 'The time has come to make an end. There are several motives. I find my pension not enough; I have therefore still to turn aside and attempt things for which people will pay. My health also counts. Asthma and other annoyances I have tolerated for years; but I cannot put up with cancer . . .' He had always held a brief for suicide, proclaiming his belief in talk and writing. On the 23rd of March 'he left his home never to return: nearly six months afterwards his body was discovered by some fishermen in

[1] *The Brave Days* by Neil Munro

Mount's Bay, and, in accordance with his known wishes, was buried at sea'.[1] Davidson certainly anticipated his end, just as Dylan Thomas did, in his own verse:

> I felt the world a spinning on its nave,
> I felt it sheering blindly round the sun;
> I felt the time had come to find a grave:
> I knew it in my heart my days were done.
> I took my staff in hand; I took the road,
> And wandered out to seek my last abode.
> Hearts of gold and hearts of lead
> Sing it yet in sun and rain,
> 'Heel and toe from dawn to dusk,
> Round the world and home again.'[2]

Davidson's poetry is curiously uneven; and even at its best seems possessed of the power to interest, rather than satisfy, the reader. It has force and drive but lacks perfection—the sense of words come finally to rest. Lionel Johnson's summary of Davidson probably remains the best critique:

> *Powerful* is the word: fervour, ardour, energy, rapid imagination and passion, sometimes heated and turbulent . . . Intensely interested in *life* and its questions: a Scotch metaphysician turned into a romantic and realistic poet, without losing his *curiosity* about things. Versatile, experimentalist, prolific: writes ballads, which are psychological problems dramatically conceived and put, with wonderful beauty of language at moments, but with a certain lack of delicacy—the poems rush and dash at you, overpower and invigorate you, rather than charm and enchant you. A restless poet —a true countryman of Burns and Carlyle, who has read the Elizabethans, and Keats and Browning. Earthly in a good sense; loves facts and Darwin:

[1] *The Eighteen Nineties* by Holbrook Jackson
[2] 'The Last Journey' (*The Testament of John Davidson*) (1908)

dreams and wonders and imagines, but always with a kind of robust consciousness. Hardest to estimate of all the younger poets: has tried so many ways and done so much. Has put genuine passion into his poetry, not an 'artistic' pose: full-blooded, generous, active: very human. Has not quite 'found himself' in literature or in life.[1]

Yeats' analysis of Davidson's failure, in much the same way, says perhaps the last word as to his limitations: 'With enough passion to make a great poet, though meeting no man of culture in early life, he lacked intellectual receptivity, and, anarchic and indefinite, lacked pose and gesture, and now no verse of his clings to my memory.'[2]

Hugh McDiarmid, who admires his later verse, has commented on Davidson's contribution to the writing of 'urban poetry' at a time when 'most of our versifiers continued to write nostalgic pseudo-pastoral rubbish about an Arcadian life which had no relation to the facts at all'.[3] There are a number of such passages scattered throughout Davidson's early verse. In the powerful but uneven dramatic poem *A Woman and Her Son*[4] there are one or two first-rate town impressions:

The working-men with heavy iron tread,
The thin-shod clerks, the shopmen neat and plump
Home from the city came. On muddy beer
The melancholy mean surburban street
Grew maudlin for an hour; pianos waked
In dissonance from dreams of rusty peace,

and

The tall lamps flickered through the sombre street,
With yellow light hiding the stainless stars:
In the next house a child awoke and cried;

[1] 'Lionel Johnson' (*Literary Essays of Ezra Pound*) (1954)
[2] 'The Tragic Generation' (*The Trembling of the Veil*)
[3] 'John Davidson: Influences and Influence' (*John Davidson: A Selection of his Poems*)
[4] *John Davidson: A Selection of his Poems*

Far off a clash and clanking trains
Broke out and ceased, as if the fettered world
Started and shook its irons in the night;
Across the dreary common citywards,
The moon among the chimneys sunk again,
Cast on the clouds a shade of smoky pearl.

The opening portions of *In the Isle of Dogs* (which gives T.S. Eliot, so he tells us, 'a fellow feeling for the poet'[1]) afford some effective metropolitan description, though Davidson's best, in this vein, is to be found in such later pieces as *The Crystal Palace* and *The Thames Embankment* (*Fleet Street and Other Poems*, 1909).

Davidson's genuine dramatic gifts were adulterated by the philosophic propaganda with which he so often mixed them. In straightforward narrative he was more felicitous, though sometimes here, too, he obscures his artistry with preaching. 'Davidson handles with marked facility', writes Bernard Muddiman, in *The Men of the Nineties*, 'the modern ballad medium of narrative verse'. *The Ballad of a Nun*, *The Ballad of an Artist's Wife*, and others, relate their story in easy jogging quatrains. As a sample one can quote from *A New Ballad of Tannhäuser*:

As he lay worshipping his bride,
  White rose leaves in her bosom fell,
On dreams came sailing on a tide
  Of sleep, he heard a matin bell.

'Hark! let us leave the magic hill,'
  He said, 'and live on earth with men.'
'No, here,' she said, 'we stay until
  The Golden Age shall come again.'

As Maurice Lindsay rightly points out 'the condition in Davidson's will which made it impossible for any new selection of his work to be published during the period of copyright has acted disastrously upon his reputation'. He and Hugh McDiarmid have campaigned vigorously on

[1] *John Davidson: A Selection of his Poems*

behalf of the virtues of Davidson's later writings. Here the impediment is the propaganda. T. S. Eliot tells us that he finds the philosophy uncongenial, and many readers will concur with his opinion. He is careful, however, to add this postscript which may stand as the last word on the poet: 'In everything that Davidson wrote I recognise a real man, to be treated not only with respect but with homage.'[1]

Hayim Fineman published a study of the poet, *John Davidson*, in 1916. There is a detailed study of his plays in Priscilla Thoules' *Modern Poetic Drama* (1934), and an account of his fiction, *John Davidson: The Novels of a Poet* by P. Turner in the *Cambridge Journal*, Vol. 5, 1952.

Thirty Bob a Week

I couldn't touch a stop and turn a screw,
  And set the blooming world a-work for me,
Like such as cut their teeth—I hope, like you—
  On the handle of a skeleton gold key;
I cut mine on a leek, which I eat it every week:
  I'm a clerk at thirty bob as you can see.

But I don't allow it's luck and all a toss;
  There's no such thing as being starred and crossed;
It's just the power of some to be a boss,
  And the bally power of others to be bossed:
I face the music, sir; you bet I ain't a cur;
  Strike me lucky if I don't believe I'm lost!

[1] *John Davidson: A Selection of his Poems*

For like a mole I journey in the dark,
  A-travelling along the underground
From my Pillar'd Halls and broad Suburbean Park,
  To come the daily dull official round;
And home again at night with my pipe all alight,
  A-scheming how to count ten bob a pound.

And it's often very cold and very wet,
  And my missis stitches towels for a hunks;
And the Pillar'd Halls is half of it to let—
  Three rooms about the size of travelling trunks.
And we cough, my wife and I, to dislocate a sigh,
  When the noisy little kids are in their bunks.

But you never hear her do a growl or whine,
  For she's made of flint and roses, very odd;
And I've got to cut my meaning rather fine,
  Or I'd blubber, for I'm made of greens and sod:
So p'r'aps we are in Hell for all that I can tell,
  And lost and damn'd and served up hot to God.

I ain't blaspheming, Mr. Silver-tongue;
  I'm saying things a bit beyond your art:
Of all the rummy starts you ever sprung,
  Thirty bob a week's the rummiest start!
With your science and your books and your the'ries
    about spooks
  Did you ever hear of looking in your heart?

I didn't mean your pocket, Mr., no:
  I mean that having children and a wife,
With thirty bob on which to come and go,
  Isn't dancing to the tabor and the fife:
When it doesn't make you drink, by Heaven! it makes
    you think,
  And notice curious items about life.

JOHN DAVIDSON

I step into my heart and there I meet
  A god-almighty devil singing small,
Who would like to shout and whistle in the street,
  And squelch the passers flat against the wall;
If the whole world was a cake he had the power to take,
  He would take it, ask for more, and eat it all.

And I meet a sort of simpleton beside,
  The kind that life is always giving beans;
With thirty bob a week to keep a bride
  He fell in love and married in his teens:
At thirty bob he stuck; but he knows it isn't luck:
  He knows the seas are deeper than tureens.

And the god-almighty devil and the fool
  That meet me in the High Street on the strike,
When I walk about my heart a-gathering wool,
  Are my good and evil angels if you like.
And both of them together in every kind of weather
  Ride me like a double-seated bike.

That's rough a bit and needs its meaning curled.
  But I have a high old hot un in my mind—
A most engrugious notion of the world,
  That leaves your lightning 'rithmetic behind
I give it at a glance when I say 'There ain't no chance,
  Nor nothing of the lucky-lottery kind.'

And it's this way that I make it out to be:
  No fathers, mothers, countries, climates—none;
Not Adam was responsible for me,
  Nor society, nor systems, nary one:
A little sleeping seed, I woke—I did, indeed—
  A million years before the blooming sun.

I woke because I thought the time had come;
  Beyond my will there was no other cause;
And everywhere I found myself at home,
  Because I chose to be the thing I was;
And in whatever shape of mollusc or of ape
  I always went according to the laws.

I was the love that chose my mother out;
  I joined two lives and from the union burst;
My weakness and my strength without a doubt
  Are mine alone for ever from the first:
It's just the very same with a difference in the name
  As 'Thy will be done.' You say it if you durst!

They say it daily up and down the land
  As easy as you take a drink, it's true;
But the difficultest go to understand,
  And the difficultest job a man can do,
Is to come it brave and meek with thirty bob a week,
  And feel that that's the proper thing for you.

It's a naked child against a hungry wolf;
  It's playing bowls upon a splutterlng wreck;
It's walking on a string across a gulf
  With millstones fore-and-aft about your neck;
But the thing is daily done by many and many a one;
  And we fall, face forward, fighting, on the deck.

JOHN DAVIDSON

Holiday at Hampton Court

Scales of pearly cloud inlay
  North and south the turquoise sky,
While the diamond lamp of day
  Quenchless burns, and time on high
A moment halts upon his way
  Bidding noon again good-bye.

Gaffers, gammers, huzzies, louts,
  Couples, gangs, and families
Sprawling, shake, with Babel-shouts
  Bluff King Hal's funereal trees;
And eddying groups of stare-abouts
  Quiz the sandstone Hercules.

When their tongues and tempers tire,
  Harry and his little lot
Condescendingly admire
  Lozenge-bed and crescent-plot,
Aglow with links of azure fire,
  Pansy and forget-me-not.

Where the emerald shadows rest
  In the lofty woodland aisle,
Chaffing lovers quaintly dressed
  Chase and double many a mile,
Indifferent exiles in the west
  Making love in cockney style.

Now the echoing palace fills;
  Men and women, girls and boys
Trample past the swords and frills,
  Kings and Queens and trulls and toys;
Or listening loll on window-sills,
  Happy amateurs of noise!

That for pictured rooms of state!
  Out they hurry, wench and knave,
Where beyond the palace-gate
  Dusty legions swarm and rave,
With laughter, shriek, inane debate,
  Kentish fire and comic stave.

Voices from the river call;
  Organs hammer tune on tune;
Larks triumphant over all
  Herald twilight coming soon,
For as the sun begins to fall
  Near the zenith gleams the moon.

JOHN DAVIDSON

Christmas Eve

BASIL, SANDY, BRIAN, MENZIES.

SANDY:

In holly hedges starving birds
  Silently mourn the setting year.

BASIL:

Upright like silver-plated swords
  The flags stand in the frozen mere.

BRIAN:

The mistletoe we still adore
  Upon the twisted hawthorn grows.

MENZIES:

In antique gardens hellebore
  Puts forth its blushing Christmas rose.

SANDY:

Shrivelled and purple, cheek by jowl,
  The hips and haws hang drearily.

BASIL:

Rolled in a ball the sulky owl
  Creeps far into his hollow tree.

BRIAN:

In abbeys and cathedrals dim
  The birth of Christ is acted o'er;
The kings of Cologne worship him,
  Balthazar, Jasper, Melchior.

MENZIES:

And while our midnight talk is made
Of this and that now and then,
The old earth-stopper with his spade
And lantern seeks the fox's den.

SANDY:

Oh, for a northern blast to blow
These depths of air that cream and curdle!

BASIL:

Now are the halcyon days, you know;
Old Time has leapt another hurdle;
And pauses as he only may
Who knows he never can be caught.

BRIAN:

The winter solstice, shortest day
And longest night, was past, I thought.

BASIL:

Oh yes! but fore-and-aft a week
Silent the winds must ever be,
Because the happy halcyons seek
Their nests upon the sea.

BRIAN:

The Christmas-time! the lovely things
That last of it! Sweet thoughts and deeds!

SANDY:

How strong and green old legend clings
Like ivy round the ruined creeds!

MENZIES:

A fearless, ruthless, wanton band,
Deep in our hearts we guard from scathe,
Of last year's log, a smouldering brand
To light at Yule the fire of faith.

BRIAN:

The shepherds in the field at night
  Beheld an angel glory-clad,
And shrank away with sore afright.
  'Be not afraid,' the angel bade.

'I bring good news to king and clown,
  To you here crouching on the sward;
For there is born in David's town
  A Saviour, which is Christ the Lord.

'Behold the babe is swathed, and laid
  Within a manger.' Straight there stood
Beside the angel all arrayed
  A heavenly multitude.

'Glory to God,' they sang; 'and peace,
  Good pleasure among men,'

SANDY:

The wondrous message of release,
  That forged another chain!

BRIAN:

Nay, nay; God help us to be good!

BASIL:

Hush! Hark! Without; the waits, the waits!
  With brass and strings, and mellow wood.

MENZIES:

  A simple tune can ope heaven's gates.

SANDY:

Slowly they play, poor careful souls,
  With wistful thoughts of Christmas cheer,
Unwitting how their music rolls
  Away the burden of the year.

BASIL:

And with the charm, the homely rune,
To early moods our minds incline,
As when our pulses beat in tune
With all the stars that shine.

MENZIES:

Oh cease! oh cease!

BASIL:

Ay, cease; and bring
The wassail-bowl, the cup of grace.

SANDY:

Pour wine, and heat it till it sing.
With cloves and cardamums and mace.

BASIL:

And frothed and sweetened round it goes,
The while we drink the whole world's health.

SANDY:

The whole world's health! But chiefly those
Who grasp the whole world's power and wealth.

BRIAN:

I drink the poor in spirit; theirs
Is heaven's kingdom.

SANDY:

Theirs, below,
A bursting granary of tares,
Derision, contumely, woe.

BRIAN:

To those who patiently have borne
Sorrow!

SANDY:

May joy come soon instead!
I drink the health of those that mourn
And never can be comforted.

BRIAN:

I drink the meek.

SANDY:

I drink their foes,
The ruthless heirs of all the earth—
The knaves, the pushing men, and those
Who claim prerogatives of birth.

BRIAN:

I drink the merciful, for they
Shall mercy gain.

SANDY:

From usurers?

BRIAN:

The pure in heart, and those who pray
And work for peace when faction stirs,
I drink; and all whom men condemn
For righteousness, who never shrink
From persecution.

SANDY:

Yes, to them!
To every sinner, too, I drink!

BASIL:

Hush! hark! the waits, far up the street!

MENZIES:

A new, unearthly charm unfolds
Of magic music wild and sweet,
Anomes and clarigolds!

A Northern Suburb

Nature selects the longest way,
  And winds about in tortuous grooves;
A thousand years the oaks decay;
  The wrinkled glacier hardly moves.

But here the whetted fangs of change
  Daily devour the old demesne—
The busy farm, the quiet grange,
  The wayside inn, the village green.

In gaudy yellow brick and red,
  With rooting pipes, like creepers rank,
The shoddy terraces o'erspread
  Meadow and garth, and daisied bank.

With shelves for rooms the houses crowd,
  Like draughty cupboards in a row—
Ice-chests when wintry winds are loud,
  Ovens when summer breezes blow.

Roused by the fee'd policeman's knock,
  And sad that day should come again,
Under the stars the workmen flock
  In haste to reach the workmen's train.

For here dwell those who must fulfil
  Dull tasks in uncongenial spheres,
Who toil through dread of coming ill,
  And not with hope of happier years—

The lowly folk who scarcely dare
  Conceive themselves perhaps misplaced,
Whose prize for unremitting care
  Is only not to be disgraced.

London

Athwart the sky a lowly sigh
  From west to east the sweet wind carried;
The sun stood still on Primrose Hill;
  His light in all the city tarried:
The clouds on viewless columns bloomed
Like smouldering lilies unconsumed.

Oh sweetheart, see! how shadowy,
  Of some occult magician's rearing,
Or swung in space of heaven's grace
  Dissolving, dimly reappearing,
Afloat upon ethereal tides
St. Paul's above the city rides!

A rumour broke through the thin smoke
  Enwreathing abbey, tower, and palace,
The parks, the squares, the thoroughfares,
  The million-peopled lanes and alleys,
An ever-muttering prisoned storm,
The heart of London beating warm.

In Romney Marsh

As I went down to Dymchurch Wall,
  I heard the South sing o'er the land;
I saw the yellow sunlight fall
  On knolls where Norman churches stand.

And ringing shrilly, taut and lithe,
  Within the wind a core of sound,
The wire from Romney town to Hythe
  Alone its airy journey wound.

A veil of purple vapour flowed
  And trailed its fringe along the Straits;
The upper air like sapphire glowed;
  And roses filled Heaven's central gates.

Masts in the offing wagged their tops;
  The swinging waves pealed on the shore;
The saffron beach, all diamond drops
  And beads of surge, prolonged the roar.

As I came up from Dymchurch Wall,
  I saw above the Downs' low crest
The crimson brands of sunset fall,
  Flicker and fade from out the west.

Night sank: like flakes of silver fire
  The stars in one great shower came down;
Shrill blew the wind; and shrill the wire
  Rang out from Hythe to Romney town.

The darkly shining salt sea drops
  Streamed as the waves clashed on the shore;
The beach, with all its organ stops
  Pealing again, prolonged the roar.

Lionel Johnson

1867-1902

LIONEL PIGOT JOHNSON was born at Broadstairs, Kent, on 15th March 1867. No formal life of him has yet been written but Iain Fletcher has contributed a model biographical and critical Introduction to his edition of Johnson's poems which, with its copious notes, is an invaluable source-book for any literary study of the 'nineties.

Johnson's parents were of mainly Celtic stock which accounts, in part, for his sympathy with the Irish cause in later life. They were Anglicans of rigid High Church principle, and Johnson's education at Winchester College provided him with a like religious background and environment. During his years there, he passed with considerable excitement through most of the higher religions and some of the 'higher atheisms'. But in the letters he wrote to his friends while he was still at school, one theme predominates: 'I will be a priest.'

From Winchester he went to New College, Oxford, and was duly influenced by the aestheticism of Walter Pater. Coming down from Oxford he took up a career of literary journalism, writing his weekly reviews with all the fastidious care of a scholar. Although he had many friends, he led an essentially bachelor existence, dwelling in two Inns of Court, and in Fitzroy Street and Clifford's

Inn. On St Alban's day 1891 he was received at St Etheldreda's into the Roman Church. Although he never took orders, the Fathers of the Church were his chief mentors, and he reported Newman as saying that he had ever regarded men-of-letters as constituting a third order of the priesthood.

From the time of his birth Johnson had been frail. 'A diminutive, ethereal creature, with a pallid beautiful face',[1] is how one friend described him. Another, recalling him, wondered how 'such knowledge and such intellectual force could be housed in so delicate a boyish frame'.[2] And along with this fragility there went an abnormally nervous organism which he strained to breaking-point by his habit of inveterate drinking.

It is possible that, from very early days, Johnson had premonitions of disaster. The poem *Mystic and Cavalier*,[3] written in 1889, with its prophetic opening line

> Go from me: I am one of those who fall

may well present us with Johnson speaking through a mask. He had certainly commenced his habit of secret and convivial drinking at Oxford, and was to write of the *Vinum Daemonium* in his poem *The Dark Angel*:[4]

> Thou art the whisper in the gloom,
> The hinting tone, the haunting laugh:
> Thou art the adorner of my tomb,
> The minstrel of mine epitaph.

Yeats has reported what seemed to him Johnson's deliberated self-destruction: '"In ten years I shall be penniless and shabby, and borrow half-crowns from friends." He seemed to contemplate a vision that gave him pleasure.'[5] Filled as he may have been with remorse,

[1] H. A. L. Fisher: *An Unfinished Autobiography* (1940)
[2] Richard Le Gallienne: *The Romantic '90's*
[3] *Poems* (1895)
[4] Ibid.
[5] 'The Tragic Generation' (*The Trembling of the Veil*)

clear-eyed, he contemplated his doom:

> The end is set:
> Though the end be not yet.[1]

Despite his alcoholism and the repressed homosexuality, from which his compulsive drinking may have sprung, Johnson's verse and prose is much less tragic than that of his friend Dowson. 'Johnson's poetry', Yeats maintained, 'conveys an emotion of joy, of intellectual clearness, of hard energy; he gave us of his triumph.'[2] This is substantially correct. He was by far the best-read man among the poets of the 'nineties; and his reading and knowledge were exquisite pleasures to him. Reviewing his critical study *The Art of Thomas Hardy*, Richard Le Gallienne had spoken of Johnson's 'remarkable, if occasionally a little oppressive'[3] learning. The poet's reply to this was characteristic and revealing: 'Doubtless I overdo quotation: but it is from mere exuberance of delight, not in any spirit of pedantry. How can one help knowing things so delightful, or making use of them.'[4]

Johnson's 'triumph', as Yeats terms it, lay in his intellectual superiority, which is to be found in the organisation of both his verse and prose. In a Preface to an edition of Johnson's poems, withdrawn very shortly after publication, Ezra Pound spoke of his sense of order. 'His language is formal,' he wrote, 'it has an old-fashioned kind of precision . . . One thinks that his poems are in short hard sentences. The reality is they are doctrinal and nearly always dogmatic. He had the blessed habit of knowing his own mind.'[5] And again, 'the impression of Lionel Johnson's verse is that of small slabs of ivory, firmly combined and contrived. There is a constant feeling of neatness, a sense of inherited order. Above all he respected his art.'[6] The

[1] 'Mystic and Cavalier' (*Poems*) (1895)
[2] 'The Tragic Generation' (*The Trembling of the Veil*)
[3] *Retrospective Reviews* (1896)
[4] *The Romantic '90's* by Richard Le Gallienne
[5] 'Lionel Johnson' (*Literary Essays of Ezra Pound*) (1954)
[6] Ibid.

weakness of his poetry is, of course, its unoriginality. 'Had there never been poets before him,' declared Le Gallienne, reviewing his verse, 'it is very unlikely that Mr. Johnson would have been a poet at all.'[1] Ezra Pound has remarked on certain of Johnson's failings—his 'treasured archaisms' and 'vain repetitions'—but it is F. W. Bateson who has delivered the most powerful critical broadside. In the thirteenth chapter of his book *English Poetry: A Critical Introduction* (1950) he prints and comments upon two poems on Oxford, one by Johnson and one by Auden, much to the disadvantage of the former.

Many of Bateson's points are well made, and Auden is, of course, the far greater poet. There is, however, too much prejudice in the essay for it to become a *locus classicus*. One might remark too that Johnson's composition is what it purports to be—a poem about Oxford, whereas Auden's work (which bears the same title) is really about nothing of the sort, but is instead a generalisation; a meditation on Nature and Wisdom. Bateson certainly fails to understand the convention within which Johnson is working. For example, he faults him for having written 'sixty lines on Oxford without once introducing the words *undergraduate*, *student*, *don*, *university*, *college*, *quadrangle*, *hall* or *library*'. What Bateson does not comprehend is that Johnson's poem is not concerned with Oxford in its administrative or sociological aspect. It is not a *realistic* but a *Platonic* account which the poet wishes to present. Johnson dedicates himself to the idea of a university,[2] and Bateson is correct in noticing how little of the personal there is in the poem. But in lamenting that instead of 'the thrill of having Walter Pater as a tutor, the charms of alcohol and Catholicism, the titillation of literary vanity', we get from Johnson only 'a versified extract from the Oxford guidebook', he has misread the poet's intention which is to celebrate the high perennial meaning of his university, not the small etceteras of its daily life:

[1] *Retrospective Reviews*

[2] John Henry Newman, one of Johnson's four literary passions, had published his addresses *The Idea of a University* in 1852

> There, Shelley dreamed his white Platonic dreams;
> There, classic Landor throve on Roman thought;
> There, Addison pursued his quiet themes;
> There, smiled Erasmus, and there, Colet taught.

It is the achievement of *these* men, and not the average undergraduate's comings and goings, which have given Oxford its peculiar humane aura, making it, as Johnson says, 'beauty's home'. The ideal, doubtless, is *out* today; but we must consent to see its validity for Johnson, if we would understand his poem aright.

'Lionel Johnson's "Oxford",' asserts Bateson, 'is a typical specimen of Romantic poetry in its Polished Craftsman and Decadent phases.' 'Decadent' here is a clear misnomer. Again and again, Johnson makes mock of the term and its coterie-associations. His short story *Incurable*[1] contains three parodies of the 'Symonsy' way of verse-writing, including *A Decadent Lyric.* To be a Decadent was, for Johnson, to be a 'slave to impressionism, whether the impression be precious or no'.[2] '*Fin-de-siècle*,' he commented scornfully, 'as the silly dialect of the day has it.'[3]

Both as a poet and as a critic he sought to resist the current Decadent flux. This he attempted by adopting a deliberate old-fashioned attitude. 'I will be loyal to loves that are not of yesterday', he wrote in *The Academy* (8th December 1900). 'New poems, new essays, new stories, new lines, are not my company at Christmastide. "My days among the dead are passed." Veracious Southey, how cruel a lie! My sole days among the dead are passed among the still-born or moribund moderns, not the white days and shining nights free for the strong voices of the ancients in fame. A classic has a permanence of pleasurability; that is the meaning of his estate and title.'

Johnson's strength is in his knowledge of the past—in part the impersonal strength of tradition. 'Every poem',

[1] *The Pageant* (1897)
[2] 'Lionel Johnson' (*The Literary Essays of Ezra Pound*)
[3] 'Friends that fail not' (*Post Liminium*) (1912)

wrote Le Gallienne, engaged in reviewing his verse, 'seems to whisper to us "the old was best" . . . and we put down the volume firmly determined to join the Legitimist League tomorrow.'[1]

During his lifetime Johnson published two works of poetry: *Poems*, 1895, and *Ireland, with other Poems*, 1897. A number of hitherto uncollected poems were included by Iain Fletcher in his edition of the poet's verse. Posthumously, there appeared two selections of criticism: *Post Liminium*, 1912; and *Reviews and Critical Papers*, 1921. Part of his scholarly correspondence was printed in 1919 under the title *Some Winchester Letters of Lionel Johnson.*

He died in London on 4th October 1902.

Plato in London

TO CAMPBELL DODGSON

The pure flame of one taper fall
Over the old and comely page:
No harsher light disturb at all
This converse with a treasured sage.
Seemly, and fair, and of the best,
 If Plato be our guest,
 Should things befall.

[1] *Retrospective Reviews*

Without, a world of noise and cold:
Here, the soft burning of the fire.
And Plato walks, where heavens unfold,
About the home of his desire.
From his own city of high things,
  He shows to us, and brings,
  Truth of fine gold.

The hours pass; and the fire burns low;
The clear flame dwindles into death:
Shut then the book with care; and so,
Take leave of Plato, with hushed breath
A little, by the falling gleams,
  Tarry the gracious dreams:
  And they too go.

Lean from the window to the air:
Hear London's voice upon the night!
Thou hast held converse with things rare:
Look now upon another sight!
The calm stars, in their living skies:
  And then, these surging cries,
  This restless glare!

That starry music, starry fire,
High above all our noise and glare:
The image of our long desire,
The beauty, and the strength, are there.
And Plato's thought lives, true and clear,
  In as august a sphere:
  Perchance, far higher.

Oxford Nights

TO VICTOR PLARR

About the august and ancient *Square*,
Cries the wild wind; and through the air,
The blue night air, blows keen and shrill:
Else, all the night sleeps, all is still.
Now, the lone *Square* is blind with gloom:
Now, on that clustering chestnut bloom,
A cloudy moonlight plays, and falls
In glory upon *Bodley*'s walls:
Now, wildlier yet, while moonlight pales,
Storm the tumultuary gales.
O rare divinity of Night!
Season of undisturbed delight:
Glad interspace of day and day!
Without, an world of winds at play:
Within, I hear what dead friends say.
Blow, winds! and round that perfect *Dome*,
Wail as you will, and sweep, and roam:
Above *Saint Mary's* carven home,
Struggle, and smite to your desire
The sainted watchers on her spire:
Or in the distance vex your power
Upon mine own *New College* tower:
You hurt not these! On me and mine,
Clear candlelights in quiet shine:
My fire lives yet! nor have I done
With *Smollett*, nor with *Richardson*:
With, gentlest of the martyrs! *Lamb*,
Whose lover I, long lover, am:
With *Gray*, whose gracious spirit knew
The sorrows of art's lonely few:

With *Fielding*, great, and strong, and tall;
Sterne, exquisite, equivocal;
Goldsmith, the dearest of them all:
While *Addison's* demure delights
Turn Oxford, into *Attic*, nights.
Still *Trim* and *Parson Adams* keep
Me better company than sleep:
Dark sleep, who loves me not; nor I
Love well her nightly death to die,
And in her haunted chapels lie.
Sleep wins me not: but from his shelf
Brings me each wit his very self:
Beside my chair the great ghosts throng,
Each tells his story, sings his song:
And in the ruddy fire I trace
The curves of each *Augustan* face.
I sit at *Doctor Primrose'* board:
I hear *Beau Tibbs* discuss a lord.
Mine, *Matthew Bramble's* pleasant wrath;
Mine, all the humours of the *Bath.*
Sir Roger and the *Man in Black*
Bring me the *Golden Ages* back.
Now white *Clarissa* meets her fate,
With virgin will inviolate:
Now *Lovelace* wins me with a smile,
Lovelace, adorable and vile.
I taste, in slow alternate way,
Letters of *Lamb*, letters of *Gray*:
Nor lives there, beneath *Oxford* towers,
More joy, than in my silent hours.
Dream, who love dreams! forget all grief,
Find, in sleep's nothingness, relief:
Better my dreams! Dear, human books,
With kindly voices, winning, looks!
Enchant me with your spells of art,
And draw me homeward to your heart:
Till weariness and things unkind

Seem but a vain and passing wind:
Till the gray morning slowly creep
Upward, and rouse the birds from sleep:
Till Oxford bells the silence break,
And find me happier, for your sake.
Then, with the dawn of common day,
Rest you! But I, upon my way,
What the fates bring, will cheerlier do,
In days not yours, through thoughts of you!

By the Statue of King Charles at Charing Cross

TO WILLIAM WATSON

Sombre and rich, the skies;
Great glooms, and starry plains.
Gently the night wind sighs;
Else a vast silence reigns.

The splendid silence clings
Around me: and around
The saddest of all kings
Crowned, and again discrowned.

Comely and calm, he rides
Hard by his own Whitehall:
Only the night wind glides:
No crowds, nor rebels, brawl.

Gone, too, his Court: and yet,
The stars his courtiers are:
Stars in their stations set;
And every wandering star.

LIONEL JOHNSON

Alone he rides, alone,
The fair and fatal king:
Dark night is all his own,
That strange and solemn thing.

Which are more full of fate:
The stars; or those sad eyes?
Which are more still and great:
Those brows; or the dark skies?

Although his whole heart yearn
In passionate tragedy:
Never was face so stern
With sweet austerity.

Vanquished in life, his death
By beauty made amends:
The passing of his breath
Won his defeated ends.

Brief life and hapless? Nay:
Through death, life grew sublime.
Speak after sentence? Yea:
And to the end of time.

Armoured he rides, his head
Bare to the stars of doom:
He triumphs now, the dead,
Beholding London's gloom.

Our wearier spirit faints,
Vexed in the world's employ:
His soul was of the saints;
And art to him was joy.

King, tried in fires of woe!
Men hunger for thy grace:
And through the night I go,
Loving thy mournful face.

Yet, when the city sleeps;
When all the cries are still:
The stars and heavenly deeps
Work out a perfect will.

The Dark Angel

Dark Angel, with thine aching lust
To rid the world of penitence:
Malicious Angel, who still dost
My soul such subtle violence!

Because of thee, no thought, no thing,
Abides for me undesecrate:
Dark Angel, ever on the wing,
Who never reaches me too late!

When music sounds, then changest thou
Its silvery to a sultry fire:
Nor will thine envious heart allow
Delight untutored by desire.

Through thee, the gracious Muses turn
To Furies, O mine Enemy!
And all the things of beauty burn
With flames of evil ecstasy.

Because of thee, the land of dreams
Becomes a gathering place of fears:
Until tormented slumber seems
One vehemence of useless tears.

LIONEL JOHNSON

When sunlight glows upon the flowers,
Or ripples down the dancing sea:
Thou, with thy troop of passionate powers,
Beleaguerest, bewilderest, me.

Within the breath of autumn woods,
Within the winter silences:
Thy venomous spirit stirs and broods,
O master of impieties!

The ardour of red flame is thine,
And thine the steely soul of ice:
Thou poisonest the fair design
Of nature, with unfair device.

Apples of ashes, golden bright;
Waters of bitterness, how sweet!
O banquet of a foul delight,
Prepared by thee, dark Paraclete!

Thou art the whisper in the gloom,
The hinting tone, the haunting laugh:
Thou art the adorner of my tomb,
The minstrel of mine epitaph.

I fight thee, in the Holy Name!
Yet, what thou dost, is what God saith:
Tempter! should I escape thy flame,
Thou wilt have helped my soul from Death:

The second Death, that never dies,
That cannot die, when time is dead:
Live Death, wherein the lost soul cries,
Eternally uncomforted.

Dark Angel, with thine aching lust!
Of two defeats, of two despairs:
Less dread, a change to drifting dust,
Than thine eternity of cares.

Do what thou wilt, thou shalt not so,
Dark Angel! triumph over me:
Lonely, unto the Lone, I go;
Divine, to the Divinity.

To Morfydd

A voice on the winds,
A voice by the waters,
  Wanders and cries:
Oh! what are the winds?
And what are the waters?
  Mine are your eyes!

Western the winds are,
And western the waters,
  Where the light lies:
Oh! what are the winds?
And what are the waters?
  Mine are your eyes?

Cold, cold grow the winds,
And wild grow the waters,
  Where the sun dies:
Oh! what are the winds?
And what are the waters?
  Mine are your eyes!

And down the night winds,
And down the night waters,
  The music flies:
Oh! what are the winds?
And what are the waters?
Cold be the winds,
And wild be the waters,
  So mine be your eyes!

Sancta Silvarum: III

TO THE EARL RUSSELL

Through the fresh woods there fleet
Fawns, with bright eyes, light feet:
Bright eyes, and feet that spurn
  The pure green fern.

Headed by leaping does,
The swift procession goes
Through thickets, over lawns:
  Followed by fawns.

Over slopes, over glades,
Down dells and leafy shades,
Away the quick deer troop:
  A wildwood group.

Under the forest airs,
A life of grace is theirs:
Courtly their look; they seem
  Things of a dream.

Some say, but who can say?
That a charmed troop are they:
Once youth and maidens white!
  These may be right.

The Age of a Dream

TO CHRISTOPHER WHALL

Imageries of dream reveal a gracious age:
Black armour, falling lace, and altar lights at morn.
The courtesy of Saints, their gentleness and scorn,
Lights on an earth more fair, than shone from Plato's
page:
The courtesy of knights, fair calm and sacred rage:
The courtesy of love, sorrow for love's sake borne.
Vanished, those high conceits! Desolate and forlorn,
We hunger against hope for that lost heritage.

Gone now, the carven work! Ruined, the golden shrine!
No more the glorious organs pour their voice divine;
No more rich frankincense drifts through the Holy Place:
Now from the broken tower, what solemn bell still tolls,
Mourning what piteous death? Answer, O saddened
souls!
Who mourn the death of beauty and the death of grace.

The Precept of Silence

I know you: solitary griefs,
Desolate passions, aching hours!
I know you: tremulous beliefs,
Agonised hopes, and ashen flowers!

The winds are sometimes sad to me;
The starry spaces, full of fear:
Mine is the sorrow of the sea,
And mine the sigh of places drear.

Some players upon plaintive strings
Publish their wistfulness abroad:
I have not spoken of these things,
Save to one man, and unto God.

The Destroyer of a Soul

TO * * * *

I hate you with a necessary hate.
First, I sought patience: passionate was she:
My patience turned in very scorn of me,
That I should dare forget a sin so great,
As this, through which I sit disconsolate;
Mourning for that live soul I used to see;
Soul of a saint, whose friend I used to be:
Till you came by! a cold, corrupting, fate.

Why come you now? You, whom I cannot cease
With pure and perfect hate to hate? Go, ring
The death-bell with a deep triumphant toll!
Say you, my friend sits by me still? Ah, peace!
Call you this thing my friend? this nameless thing?
This living body, hiding its dead soul.

A Friend

TO H. B. IRVING

All that he came to give,
He gave, and went again:
I have seen one man live,
I have seen one man reign
With all the graces in his train.

As one of us he wrought
Things of the common hour:
Whence was the charmed soul brought,
That gave each act such power;
The natural beauty of a flower?

Magnificence and grace,
Excellent courtesy:
A brightness on the face,
Airs of high memory:
Whence came all these, to such as he?

Like young Shakespearean kings,
He won the adoring throng:
And, as Apollo sings,
He triumphed with a song:
Triumphed, and sang, and passed along.

With a light word, he took
The hearts of men in thrall:
And, with a golden look,
Welcomed them, at his call
Giving their love, their strength, their all.

No man less proud than he,
Nor cared for homage less:
Only, he could not be
Far off from happiness:
Nature was bound to his success.

Weary, the cares, the jars,
The lets, of every day:
But the heavens filled with stars,
Chanced he upon the way:
And where he stayed, all joy would stay.

Now, when sad night draws down,
When the austere stars burn:
Roaming the vast live town,
My thoughts and memories yearn
Towards him, who never will return.

Yet have I see him live,
And owned my friend, a king:
All that he came to give,
He gave: and I, who sing
His praise, bring all I have to bring.

Doctor Major

TO DR BIRBECK HILL

Why, no Sir! If a barren rascal cries,
That he is most in love with pleasing woe,
'Tis plain, Sir! what to think of him: We know
The dog lies; and the dog, too, knows he lies.
Sir! if he's happy, he will dry his eyes,
And stroll at Vauxhall for an hour or so:
If he's unhappy, it were best he go
Hang himself straight, nor pester us with sighs.

Enough, Sir! Let us have no more of it:
Your friend is little better than a Whig.
But you and I, Sir, who are men of wit,
Laugh at the follies of a canting prig.
Let those who will, Sir! to such whims submit:
No, Sir! we'll to the *Mitre*: Frank! my wig,

Oxford

TO ARTHUR GALTON

Over, the four long years! And now there rings
One voice of freedom and regret: *Farewell!*
Now old remembrance sorrows, and now sings:
But song from sorrow, now, I cannot tell.

City of weathered cloister and worn court;
Gray city of strong towers and clustering spires:
Where art's fresh loveliness would first resort;
Where lingering art kindled her latest fires.

Where on all hands, wondrous with ancient grace,
Grace touched with age, rise works of goodliest men:
Near Wykeham's art obtain their splendid place
The zeal of Inigo, the strength of Wren.

Where at each coign of every antique street,
A memory hath taken root in stone:
There, Raleigh shone; there, toiled Franciscan feet;
There, Johnson flinched not, but endured, alone.

There, Shelley dreamed his white Platonic dreams;
There, classic Landor throve on Roman thought;
There, Addison pursued his quiet themes;
There, smiled Erasmus, and there, Colet taught.

And there, O memory more sweet than all!
Lived he, whose eyes keep yet our passing light;
Whose crystal lips Athenian speech recall;
Who wears Rome's purple with least pride, most right.

There is the Oxford, strong to charm us yet:
Eternal in her beauty and her past.
What, though her soul be vexed? She can forget
Cares of an hour: only the great things last.

Only the gracious air, only the charm,
The ancient might of true humanities:
These, nor assault of man, nor time, can harm;
Nor these, nor Oxford with her memories.

Together have we walked with willing feet
Gardens of plenteous trees, bowering soft lawn:
Hills, whither Arnold wandered; and all sweet
June meadows, from the troubling world withdrawn:

Chapels of cedarn fragrance, and rich gloom
Poured from empurpled panes on either hand:
Cool pavements, carved with legends of the tomb;
Grave haunts, where we might dream and understand.

Over, the four long years! And unknown powers
Call to us, going forth upon our way:
Ah! turn we, and look back upon the towers,
That rose about our lives, and cheered the day.

Proud and serene, against the sky, they gleam:
Proud and secure, upon the earth, they stand:
Our city hath the air of a pure dream,
And hers indeed is an Hesperian land.

Think of her so! the wonderful, the fair,
The immemorial, and the ever young:
The city, sweet with our forefather's care;
The city, where the Muses all have sung.

Ill times may be; she hath no thought of time:
She reigns beside the waters yet in pride.
Rude voices cry: but in her ears the chime
Of full, sad bells brings back her old springtide.

Like to a queen in pride of place, she wears
The splendour of a crown in Radcliffe's dome.
Well fare she, well! As perfect beauty fares;
And those high places, that are beauty's home.

W. B. Yeats

1865–1939

WILLIAM BUTLER YEATS was born on 13th June 1865 at Sandymount, near Dublin, the son of an attorney of Protestant family, who later became an artist.

There have been many good and full biographies of Yeats, among which should be noted Richard Ellman's two studies: *Yeats: The Man and the Masks* (1948), and Norman Jeffares' *W. B. Yeats: Man and Poet* (1949). But for Yeats' relations with the poets of the 'nineties, and the thought and intentions behind his verse until the turn of the century, the most important documents are his own *Autobiographies* first published in 1926. These consist of two separate works, *Reveries over Childhood and Youth* (1914) and *The Trembling of the Veil* (1922); the second of these providing us with an indispensable source-book for studying the poets of the 'nineties.

Yeats was educated at several schools in Dublin and London, in which latter city much of his childhood was spent. He many times lamented that he 'lacked scholarship', believing that the traditional learning attained at a university would have set his mind at rest. Instead, he had attended art school from 1883 to 1886, though aware all the time that it was literature and reading which exercised the stronger fascination for him. When, in 1891, he met the other members of the Rhymers Club, he became aware of the particular bias which his own education had given him, and how it differed from that of those who had received more academic training. 'I was', he tells us, 'full of thought, often very abstract thought, longing all the while to be full of images, because I had gone to the art school instead of a university.'[1]

The form which Yeats' education had taken was probably a gain to him as a poet. He tells us how he 'began to pray that [his] imagination might somehow be rescued from abstraction and become as preoccupied with life as had been the imagination of Chaucer'.[2] He was, in fact, only content when his 'abstractions had composed themselves into picture and dramatisation'.[3] If this led to a deficiency of 'thought-content' in his early verses through his refusal to permit them 'any share of an intellect which I considered impure',[4] at least it kept his poetry concrete, guarding against that vague and excitable diction of liberal idealism to be found in much late-Victorian verse. Yeats was certainly lucky to escape the kind of poetic Hegelianism to which such 'generalizing' poets as Robert Bridges and Lascelles Abercrombie in their more ambitious efforts succumbed. It is revealing in this connection to compare two poems by Yeats and Abercrombie in both of which the poets are concerned with enunciating their themes and intentions in broad terms against a broad background. Here are the first lines from Abercrombie's poem *Epilogue*:

> What shall we do for Love these days?
> How shall we make an altar-blaze
> To smite the horny eyes of men
> With the renown of our Heaven,
> And to the unbelievers prove
> Our service to our dear god, Love?

[1] 'Four Years: 1887–1891' (*The Trembling of the Veil*)
[2] 'Four Years: 1887–1891' (*The Trembling of the Veil*)
[3] Ibid.
[4] Ibid.

What torches shall we lift above
The crowd that pushes through the mire,
To amaze the dark heads with strange fire?
I should think I were much to blame,
If never I held some fragrant flame
Above the noises of the world,
And openly 'mid men's hurrying stares,
Worshipt before the sacred fears
That are like flashing curtains furl'd
Across the presence of our Lord Love.

And here the first two stanzas from Yeats' epilogue to his book *The Rose* (1893):

TO IRELAND IN THE COMING TIMES

Know, that I would accounted be
True brother of that company,
Who sang to sweeten Ireland's wrong,
Ballad and story, rann and song;
Nor be I any less of them,
Because the red-rose-bordered hem
Of her, whose history began
Before God made the angelic clan,
Trails all about the written page.
When time began to rant and rage
The measure of her flying feet
Made Ireland's heart begin to beat;
And Time bade all his candles flare
To light a measure here and there;
And may the thoughts of Irelands brood
Upon a measured quietude.

Nor may I less be counted one
With Davis, Mangan, Ferguson,
Because to him, who ponders well,
My rhymes more than their rhyming tell
Of things discovered in the deep,
Where only body's laid asleep.

For the elemental creatures go
About my table to and fro,
That hurry from unmeasured mind
To rant and rage in flood and wind;
Yet he who treads in measured ways
May surely barter gaze for gaze.
Man ever journeys on with them
After the red-rose-bordered hem.
Ah, faeries, dancing under the moon,
A Druid land, a Druid tune!

There are, of course, non-concrete references in the poem; but Yeats is successful where Abercrombie is not, in implicating what is impalpable with what is sensuous, of the physical world. For example, the Irish goddess-figure is effectively 'realised' in a way that Abercrombie's 'Love' is not, by rendering her invisibility in partly visible terms: 'the red-rose-bordered hem' which 'Trails all about the written page'. In a similar fashion, Yeats presents 'the elemental beings' which go 'About my table to and fro'. This is to give these essences of thought 'local habitation' if not, indeed, a name. Yeats in missing the university education which Abercrombie enjoyed, avoided receiving that academic shorthand, that built-in reference to Platonism, which humanistic learning provides. Because of this he was largely forced to elaborate a tradition for himself, and for all the short-comings of this self-taught system, his language is the gainer in that there is more of the first-hand about it. It is this thinking in images which imparts so much life to Yeats' early essays, preserving them from the decay which overtakes the out-dated academic. How pregnant, for instance, is his image of Shaw with his 'inorganic' style of 'logical straightness' as 'a sewing machine, that clicked and shone' and which 'smiled, smiled perpetually'.[1]

Yeats' considerable intellectual powers are to be found in his early essays *Images of Good and Evil* (1904) rather

[1] 'The Tragic Generation' (*The Trembling of the Veil*)

than in his two plays *The Countess Cathleen* (1892), *The Land of Heart's Desire* (1894), his selection of lyrics which appeared with the first of these dramas under the title of *The Rose*, *The Wind among the Reeds* (1899), and his volume of sketches, anecdotes, and tales *The Celtic Twilight* (1893). Richard Le Gallienne recalled how literary London of the 'nineties was 'like a series of booths at a fair, each with its vociferous "barker" inviting us in to the only show on earth'. In one of these W.E. Henley (editor of the *National Observer*) 'was beating the big-drum of Imperialism supported by a band of brilliant young literary swordsmen'. 'Another mystic-looking booth,' he continued, 'flying a green flag with an Irish harp figured upon it, was presided over by a cabalistic young poet, Mr. W. B. Yeats, musically talking of Rosicrucianism, fairies, Celtic folklore, and an Irish theatre, and backed by Irish scholars proclaiming the revival of the Gaelic tongue as the certain cure-all for Ireland's wrongs.'[1]

All this sounds more picturesque than intellectually stimulating, and there is a great deal of what the pragmatic Anglo-Saxon might consider naive or sloppy thinking in the pieces which make up *The Celtic Twilight* ('No matter what one doubts, one never doubts the faeries, for, as the man with the Mohawk Indian on his arm said, "they stand to reason".'—'Belief and Unbelief'.) But the manner in which Yeats tackled the task of providing this Celtic movement with an adequate poetry was anything but vague and sentimental.

Two years after his first book of verse made up of the long narrative poem *The Wandering of Usheen* and the lyrics entitled *Crossways*, he founded in 1891 the National Literary Society which seven years later brought into existence the Irish Literary Theatre at Dublin.

Patriotism may be a virtue and yet cover a multitude of vices. So, at least, Yeats was to discover in his researches into the muse of his race. As member of a Young Ireland Society, he recalled how he had 'paid honour to the Irish

[1] *The Romantic '90's*

poets who wrote in English',[1] having then no knowledge of Gaelic. 'I knew in my heart', he admitted, 'that most of them wrote badly, and yet such romance clung about them, such a desire for Irish poetry was in all our minds, that I kept on saying . . . that most of them wrote well, or all but well.'[2] He could not, however, hide the truth from himself indefinitely. Looking back in 1925, he recognised that 'The Irish form of Victorian rhetoric had declined into a patriotic extravagance that offended all educated minds.'[3] This statement is probably expressed with the emphasis and clarification of hind-sight. The question for Yeats in the 'nineties was—what to do for poetry in Ireland? 'I thought one day,' he relates, ' "If somebody could make a style which would not be an English style and yet would be musical and full of colour, many others would catch fire from him, and we would have a really great school of ballad poetry in Ireland.' "[4] The style 'not English' which Yeats at length achieved was the result of a rare combination: the *matter* of Celtic folk-lore and legend, and the *manner* of French symbolism. Such a formulation may be thought to over-simplify: at least it defines in a rough and ready way some of the characteristic effects of the poems in his book *The Wind among the Reeds* (1899)

HE MOURNS FOR THE CHANGE THAT HAS COME UPON HIM AND HIS BELOVED AND LONGS FOR THE END OF THE WORLD

Do you not hear me calling, white deer with no horns?
I have been changed to a hound with one red ear;
I have been in the Path of Stones and the Wood of
  Thorns,
For somebody hid hatred and hope and desire and fear
Under my feet that they follow you night and day.

[1] 'What is "Popular Poetry"?' (*Essays and Introductions*) (1961)
[2] Ibid.
[3] 'Dedication' to *Early Poems and Stories*
[4] 'What is "Popular Poetry"?' (*Essays and Introductions*)

A man with a hazel wand came without sound;
He changed me suddenly; I was looking another way;
And now my calling is but the calling of a hound;
And Time and Birth and Change are hurrying by:
I would that the Boar without bristles had come from
  the West
And had rooted the sun and moon and stars out of the
  sky
And lay in the darkness, grunting, and turning to his
  rest.

The theory on which this achievement was based is interesting and worth considering. In his essay 'What is "Popular Poetry"?' (1907), Yeats distinguished between three important species: 'Poetry of the coteries'; 'poetry of the people'; and, thirdly, 'popular poetry'. The first is a poetry made with care. It is literary and highly conscious, and presupposes, for author and reader, the existence of a *written* tradition. The second is a poetry full of 'ancient technicalities and mysteries', and presupposes, for speaker and hearer, the existence of an *unwritten* tradition. 'Both are alike strange and obscure, and unreal to all who have not understanding, and both, instead of that manifest logic, that clear rhetoric of the "popular poetry", glimmer with thoughts and images whose "ancestors were stout and wise".' It is only the third, 'popular poetry' (a poetry never made by the people but by 'the poets of a predominant portion of the middle-class': Longfellow, Macaulay, Mrs Hemans) which does not presuppose more than it says. 'Longfellow has his popularity . . . because he tells his story or his idea so one needs nothing but his verses to understand him.' Yeats, from his experience of studying bad translations from the Irish in libraries, and sitting by turf fires in Connach to hear the telling of folk-lore and tales, learned to combine in his verse the *written* and *unwritten* traditions. What better description of symbolist verse than *poetry which presupposes more than it says!*

W. B. YEATS

Yeats' greater poetry, composed many years after the 'nineties, has largely monopolized critical attention. Writing in 1925 of verse belonging to the century's last decade, he records how he has 'had to go through it all, cutting out or altering passages that [were] sentimental from lack of thought'.[1] Yeats was, in fact, a tireless reviser; and there is a fascinating essay, 'The Later Yeats', by Sir Herbert Read in *A Coat of Many Colours* (1945) in which he compares in detail the 1893 version of *The Sorrows of Love* with the 1933 re-writing. The changes, he remarks, are all in favour of the concrete and the specific.

Yeats' own severe later attitude to his early embroidered verse—'there's more enterprise/In walking naked'[2]—has confirmed contemporary critics in their preoccupation with 'the fascination of what's difficult'[3] in the poet. No doubt he was right in finding in certain early works of his 'a slight sentimental sensuality which is disagreeable'.[4] Even so, there are poems written 'in the simplest language'[5] by him in the 'nineties which would largely satisfy our present demand for natural unstrained language. *The Lamentation of the Old Pensioner*, *The Song of the Old Mother*, and, to a lesser extent, *The Fiddler of Dooney* go a long way towards that innocence 'which is the highest achievement of the human intellect'. Here are three lines from the first:

> And the young lie long and dream in their bed
> Of the matching of ribbons for bosom and head,
> And their day goes over in idleness.

and here, four lines from the third:

> For the good are always merry
> Save by an evil chance,
> And the merry love the fiddle,
> And the merry love to dance.

[1] 'Dedication' to *Early Poems and Stories*
[2] 'A Coat' (*Responsibilities*) (1914)
[3] *The Green Helmet and Other Poems* (1910)
[4] 'The Tragic Generation' (*The Trembling of the Veil*)
[5] 'Dedication' to *Early Poems and Stories*

Symons, a friend of Yeats in the 'nineties, wrote in a review of *The Wind among the Reeds*: 'Mr. Yeats is the only one among the younger English poets who has the whole poetical temperament, and nothing but the poetical temperament.'[1]

Since the poet's death on 28th January 1939 there have been numerous studies of his work, among which may be mentioned T. R. Henn's *The Lonely Tower: Studies in the Poetry of W. B. Yeats* (1950), and P. Ure's *Towards a Mythology: Studies in the Poetry of Yeats* (1946). G. S. Fraser's monograph on *W. B. Yeats* (1954) in the British Council *Writers and Their Work* series offers an interesting brief survey. There is a fictionalised portrait of Yeats (as the musician Ulick Dean) in George Moore's novel *Evelyn Innes* (1898) written when the poet was his friend, followed by a vividly malicious one in *Hail & Farewell* (1925) Moore's autobiography, when the two men had become enemies.

[1]'Mr. W. B. Yeats' (1900, 1904), reprinted in *Studies in Prose and Verse* (1904)

The Song of the Old Mother

I rise in the dawn, and I kneel and blow
Till the seed of the fire flicker and glow;
And then I must scrub and bake and sweep
Till stars are beginning to blink and peep;
And the young lie long and dream in their bed
Of the matching of ribbons for bosom and head,
And their day goes over in idleness,
And they sigh if the wind but lift a tress;
While I must work because I am old,
And the seed of the fire gets feeble and cold.

The Moods

Time drops in decay,
Like a candle burnt out,
And the mountains and woods
Have their day, have their day;
What one in the rout
Of the fire-born moods
Has fallen away?

The Lamentation of the Old Pensioner[1]

Although I shelter from the rain
Under a broken tree,
My chair was nearest to the fire
In every company
That talked of love or politics,
Ere Time transfigured me.

Though lads are making pikes again
For some conspiracy,
And crazy rascals rage their fill
At human tyranny,
My contemplations are of Time
That has transfigured me.

There's not a woman turns her face
Upon a broken tree,
And yet the beauties that I loved
Are in my memory;
I spit into the face of Time
That has transfigured me.

[1] Since its first appearance in *The Rose* (1893) this poem underwent much change. The present text is taken from *Early Poems and Stories* (1925)

The Fiddler of Dooney

When I play my fiddle in Dooney,
Folk dance like a wave of the sea;
My cousin is priest in Kilvarnet,
My brother in Mocharabuiee.

I passed my brother and cousin:
They read in their books of prayer;
I read in my book of songs
I bought at the Sligo fair.

When we come at the end of time
To Peter sitting in state,
He will smile at the three old spirits,
But call me first through the gate;

For the good are always merry,
Save by an evil chance,
And the merry love the fiddle,
And the merry love to dance:

And when the folk there spy me,
They will all come up to me,
With 'Here is the fiddler of Dooney!'
And dance like a wave of the sea.

When You Are Old

When you are old and gray and full of sleep,
And nodding by the fire, take down this book,
And slowly read, and dream of the soft look
Your eyes had once, and of their shadows deep;

How many loved your moments of glad grace,
And loved your beauty with love false or true;
But one man loved the pilgrim soul in you,
And loved the sorrows of your changing face.

And bending down beside the glowing bars
Murmur, a little sadly, how love fled
And paced upon the mountains overhead
And hid his face among a crowd of stars.

He Hears the Cry of the Sedge

I wander by the edge
Of this desolate lake
Where wind cries in the sedge:
Until the axle break
That keeps the stars in their round,
And hands hurl in the deep
The banners of East and West,
And the girdle of light is unbound,
Your breast will not lie by the breast
Of your beloved in sleep.

He Thinks of Those who have spoken Evil of his Beloved

Half close your eyelids, loosen your hair,
And dream about the great and their pride;
They have spoken against you everywhere,
But weigh this song with the great and their pride;
I made it out of a mouthful of air,
Their children's children shall say they have lied.

John Gray

1866–1934

JOHN GRAY was born on 10th March 1866 at Woolwich. As a boy, he joined the Roman Church and entered the priesthood at the age of thirty-five. Details of his life are to be found in *The Aylesford Review* edited by Father Brocard Sewell, O.Carm. (Vol. 4, No. 2, Spring 1961) and in book-form under the title of *Two Friends: Canon Gray and Mr Raffalovich* published as a limited edition by the St Albert's Press.

Talented and good-looking, Gray was fortunate as a young man in winning the attention of Oscar Wilde who shouldered the expense of bringing out *Silverpoints* (1892), his first volume of verse. When the *Daily Telegraph* made some comment on Gray as a 'discovery' or protégé of Wilde, the latter replied in a letter to the editor that he had sought Gray's acquaintance 'because he had already a perfected mode of expression both in prose and verse'.[1] Inaccurately, rumour had it that Gray was the original of the character Dorian Gray in Wilde's sensational novel. Certainly, he had the highest regard for him; and, writing to Lord Alfred Douglas in his great *De Profundis* letter, Wilde contrasted these two young men of charm, one as industrious as the other was idle: 'When I compare my friendship with you with such still younger men as John

[1] 19th February 1892. *The Letters of Oscar Wilde*, ed. Rupert Hart-Davis

Gray and Pierre Louys, I feel ashamed. My real life, my higher life was with them and such as they.'[1]

Besides the admiration and goodwill of Wilde, Gray was lucky in possessing the support of André Raffalovich, his life-long friend, a rich Russian Jew who, as Wilde put it, had come to this country to establish a *salon* and succeeded only in founding a saloon. Raffalovich and Wilde fell out over a frivolous remark which Wilde had made in reviewing a volume of verse by the former. Incensed at the slighting treatment, Raffalovich was successful in breaking up the friendship between Wilde and Gray; and when the latter entered the Roman priesthood Raffalovich built him St Peter's Church in Edinburgh.

Gray, as a poet of the 'nineties, is associated always with the one book *Silverpoints* 'published at the Sign of the Bodley Head in Vigo Street'. This wafer-slim volume of thirty-eight pages, limited to 250 copies, bore as an epigraph these words from Paul Verlaine: 'en composant des acrostiches indolents'—fitting superscription for a work so consciously recherché in production and expression. Between its green and powdered gold covers, it contained twenty-nine poems, of which sixteen were original and thirteen were translations from the French (seven from Verlaine, one from Mallarmé, two from Rimbaud, and three from Baudelaire). Osbert Burdett, in his book *The Beardsley Period*, gives a good account of *Silverpoints*:

> This slim volume which is almost the shape of a cheque-book standing on its end has several points of interest. It is printed in a minute italic relieved by Roman capital initials, occasionally themselves set in a decoration. Most of the poems are inscribed, among others, to Verlaine, Oscar Wilde, Ellen Terry, R. H. Sherard, Charles Shannon and Ernest Dowson. Altogether, in appearance, inspiration, intention, style and subject, it is a very characteristic volume. The verse is that of an accomplished craftsman, very

[1] *Letters of Oscar Wilde*

> much in his own movement, who can write but cannot sing. It is the curiosities of the pen, not the subtleties of the heart, that he reveals, seeking to intensify the convention then in fashion . . . He is often considered as obscure, but always scholarly in manner. Domination is a word of five syllables to him, and when he rhymes heart and spikenard we know that the flaw seemed lovely to him. He does not hesitate to distribute the word sun-beam between two lines, or to begin a line with the last word of a sentence . . . Carelessness can never accomplish experiments like these, which are the careful licences of the craftsman . . . The skill is undeniable, but does it touch anything deeper than critical interest and curiosity?

Reviewing the volume in March 1893, Richard Le Gallienne associated its author with the so-called Decadents, and engaged in gentle raillery at the poet's expense. Quoting from a poem the following lines:

> In every kiss I call you mine,
> Tell me, my dear, how pure, how brave
> Our child will be! What velvet eyne,
> What bonny hair our child will have?

he asked, 'Is not this absurdly domestic in a decadent? Really, Mr. Gray must check these natural impulses.'[1] He was, however, prepared to concede that the poet possessed 'a gift of epithet, of dainty colour, and subtle rhythm such as distinguish his *Silverpoints* from any recent English poetry'.[2] He also found in the book a 'quaint deliciousness' which reminded him of 'certain old English poets'.

This last quality certainly indicated a predisposition and sympathy in Gray; and in 1896 he produced an edition of Michael Drayton's *Nymphidia and the Muses Elizium*. Like *Silverpoints*, this work also came before the world with all a limited edition title's special pride in its appearance. As the end-paper of the volume proclaimed, it was

[1] *Retrospective Reviews* (1896)
[2] Ibid.

'decorated with woodcut frontispiece and border done by Charles Ricketts, under whose supervision the book has been printed at the Ballantyne Press'. Gray is very much a collector's poet.

Considered without typographical support, Gray is a less significant figure. His true stature is probably given by Lionel Johnson, writing to Katherine Tynan: 'a sometimes beautiful oddity: not more'.[1]

Gray possessed the poet's true curiosity—a desire to subject to artistic expression subjects and experience hitherto uncovered. His poem *The Forge* (which appeared in *The Savoy* for April 1896) is a good illustration of this. His description of the workers preparing their snack seeks originality of diction and yet fails in its over-all effect:

The anvil polished bright,
With leather skirt, two hearty chunks of bread,
Protecting ivory bacon, purple veined,

Are set therein with caution; and the wight
Who owns the morsel, passes over it
A piece of red-hot iron till 'tis brown.
It clears the tongue to hear it fizzle and spit,
If two hours' work vouchsafe no appetite.

Gray had been accused with Theodore Wratislawe (a rather Symons-esque poet) of fiddling their amours around the town. By the end of the 'nineties, however, his synthetic concoction of 'tigress's blood and tiger-lilies'[2] had given way to religious conventionalities, of which the following will certainly suffice:

The holy night that Christ was born
The ox stood reverently apart,
Both ruminating eaten corn,
And pondering within his heart.[3]

In 1896, he published *Spiritual Poems*, a book much

[1] *The Literary Essays of Ezra Pound*
[2] Bernard Muddiman: *The Men of the 'Nineties*
[3] 'The Ox' (*Pageant*) (1896)

prized by his friend Beardsley which, with a few others, the latter retained when Leonard Smithers sold his library for him. 'You might', he wrote to the publisher, 'get Zaensdorf [sic] or someone to put [it] into a scarlet maroquin cover for me.'[1]

Gray's name and Beardsley's are closely associated. The latter's interest in Roman Catholicism and his reception into the Roman Church owed much to Gray, a Catholic since boyhood. At one time Beardsley was financially supported by Gray's friend Raffalovich, to whom he wrote often in his final years. This correspondence was edited by Gray and published as *The Last Letters of Aubrey Beardsley* in 1915.

Before he entered the priesthood, Gray proved a versatile writer. In 1892 the Independent Theatre staged his rhymed version of Théophile Gautier's play *Le Baiser* at the Royalty, in a programme of three 'one-acters' which included *The Minister's Call* by Arthur Symons and *A Visit* by Edward Brandes adapted by William Archer. This was followed in 1893 by *The Blackmailers*, written in collaboration with Raffalovich. He also wrote a number of short stories, two of which, *Niggard Truth* and *Light*, appearing in the *Pageant* for 1896 and 1897, show his interest in the psychology of belief.

There is a good essay entitled 'The Poetry of John Gray' by Iain Fletcher in the issue of *The Aylesford Review* already cited.

Canon John Gray died at Edinburgh on 16th June 1934.

The Barber

I dreamed I was a barber; and there went
Beneath my hand, oh! manes extravagant.
Beneath my trembling fingers, many a mask
Of many a pleasant girl. It was my task

[1] *Letters from Aubrey Beardsley to Leonard Smithers*

JOHN GRAY

To gild their hair, carefully, strand by strand;
To paint their eyebrows with a timid hand;
To draw a bodkin, from a vase of kohl,
Through the closed lashes; pencils from a bowl
Of sepia to paint them underneath;
To blow upon their eyes with a soft breath.
Then lay them back and watch the leaping bands.

The dream grew vague. I moulded with my hands
The mobile breasts, the valleys; and the waist
I touched; and pigments reverently placed
Upon their thighs in sapient spots and stains,
Beryls and crysolites and diaphanes,
And gems whose hot harsh names are never said.
I was a masseur; and my fingers bled
With wonder as I touched their awful limbs.

Suddenly, in the marble trough, there seems
O, last of my pale mistresses, Sweetness!
A twy-lipped scarlet pansy. My caress
Tinges thy steel-gray eyes to violet.
Adown thy body skips the pit-a-pat
Of treatment once heard in a hospital
For plagues that fascinate, but half appal.

So, at the sound, the blood of one stood cold.
The chaste hair ripened into sudden gold.
The throat, the shoulders, swelled and were uncouth;
The breasts rose up and offered each a mouth.
And on the belly pallid blushes crept.
That maddened me, until I laughed and wept.

Mishka

TO HENRI TEIXERIA DE MATTOS

Mishka is poet among the beasts.
When roots are rotten, and rivers weep,
The bear is at play in the land of sleep.
Though his head be heavy between his fists.
The bear is poet among the beasts.

THE DREAM:

Wide and large are the monster's eyes,
Nought saying, save one word alone:
Mishka!

Mishka! Mishka! as turned to stone,
Hears no word else, nor in anywise
Can see aught save the monster's eyes.

Honey is under the monster's lips;
And Mishka follows into her lair,
Dragged in the net of her yellow hair,
Knowing all things when honey drops
On his tongue like rain, the song of the hips.

Of the honey-child, and of each twin mound.
Mishka! there screamed a far bird-note,
Deep in the sky, when round his throat
The triple coil of her hair she wound.
And stroked his limbs with a humming sound.

Mishka is white like a hunter's son;
For he knows no more of the ancient south
When the honey-child's lips are on his mouth,
When all her kisses are joined in one,
And his body is bathed in grass and sun.

JOHN GRAY

JE PLEURS DANS LES COINS; JE N'AI PLUS GOÛT À RIEN; OH! J'AI TANT PLEURÉ, DIMANCHE, EN MOI PAROISSIEN!—Jules Laforgue

Did we not, Darling, you and I,
Walk on the earth like other men?
Did we not walk and wonder why
They spat upon us so. And then

We lay us down among fresh earth,
Sweet flowers breaking overhead,
Sore needed rest for our frail girth,
For our frail hearts; a well-sought bed.

So Spring came and spread daffodils;
Summer, and fluffy bees sang on;
The fluffy bee knows us, and fills
His house with sweet to think upon.

Deep in the dear dust, Dear, we dream.
Our melancholy is a thing
At last our own; and none esteem
How our black lips are blackening.

And none note how our poor eyes fall,
Nor how our cheeks are sunk and sere.
Dear, when you waken, will you call?
Alas! we are not very near.

Lean Back and Press the Pillow Deep

AINSI, ELLE VIENDRAIT À MOI! LES YEUX BIEN FOUS!
ET ELLE ME SUIVRAIT AVEC CET AIR PARTOUT!

Lean back, and press the pillow deep,
Heart's dear demesne, dear Daintiness;
Close your tired eyes, but not to sleep . . .
How very pale your pallor is!

You smile, your cheek's voluptuous line
Melts in your dimple's saucy cave.
Your hairbraids seem a wilful vine,
Scorning to imitate a wave.

Your voice is tenebrous, as if
An angel mocked a blackbird's pipe.
You are my magic orchard feoff,
Where bud and fruit are always ripe.

O apple garden! all the days
Are fain to crown the darling year.
Ephemeral bells and garland bays,
Shy blade and lusty, bursting ear.

In every kiss I call you mine,
Tell me, my dear, how pure, how brave
Our child will be! what velvet eyne,
What bonny hair our child will have!

Sensation

IMITATED FROM THE FRENCH OF ARTHUR RIMBAUD

I walk the alleys trampled through the wheat,
Through whole blue summer eves, on velvet grass.
Dreaming, I feel the dampness at my feet.
The breezes bathe my naked head and pass.

I do not think a simple thought, nor say
A word; but in my soul the mists upcurl
Of infinite love. I will go far away
With nature, happily, as with a girl.

Charleville

IMITATED FROM THE FRENCH OF ARTHUR RIMBAUD
TO FRANK HARRIS

The square, with gravel paths and shabby lawns.
Correct, the trees and flowers repress their yawns.
The tradesman brings his favourite conceit
To air it, while he stifles with the heat.

In the kiosk, the military band.
The shakos nod the time of the quadrilles.
The flaunting dandy strolls about the stand.
The notary, half conscious of his seals

On the green seats, small groups of grocermen
Absorbed, their sticks scooping a little hole
Upon the path, talk market prices; then
Take up a cue: I think, upon the whole . . .

The loutish roughs are larking in the grass.
The sentimental trooper, with a rose
Between his teeth, seeing a baby, grows
More tender, with an eye upon the nurse.

Unbuttoned, like a student, I follow
A couple of girls along the chesnut row.
They know I am following, for they turn and laugh,
Half impudent, half shy, inviting chaff.

I do not say a word, I only stare
At their round fluffy necks. I follow where
The shoulders droop; I struggle to define
The subtle torso's hesitating line.

Only my rustling tread, deliberate, slow;
The rippled silence from the still leaves drips.
They think I am an idiot, they speak low;
—I feel faint kisses creeping on my lips.

JOHN GRAY

RICHARD LE GALLIENNE

Richard Le Gallienne

1866-1947

RICHARD LE GALLIENNE was born on 20th January 1866, in Liverpool, the eldest son of a brewery manager whose ancestors hailed from the Channel Islands.

His own autobiography *The Romantic '90's* (1926), while giving a fascinating picture of the period, is sadly deficient in personal facts. There is, however, a short account of his career in H. Montgomery Hyde's Introduction to the 1951 edition of that work.[1]

Le Gallienne was a born charmer, 'the golden boy of the 1890's'.[2] Failing an accountancy examination, he charmed Wilson Barrett, the famous actor-manager who gave him a part in one of his productions and made him, for a short time, his secretary. Established in the capital, he next charmed T.P. O'Connor, editor of *The Star*, who gave him review work to do which appeared over the signature 'Log-roller'. John Lane, publisher at The Bodley Head, then proceeded to make him his reader. As Le Gallienne candidly admitted, 'A young man who is at once a reviewer for a great newspaper and a publisher's reader will not long remain without friends.'[3] Oscar Wilde, arbiter and patron of the poets of the 'nineties, was now numbered among

[1] See also *The Quest of the Golden Boy* by R. Whittington-Egan and G. Smerdon, 1960

[2] *The Complete Poems of Lionel Johnson*, ed. Iain Fletcher

[3] *The Romantic '90's*

them, having fallen a victim to Le Gallienne's mixture of charm and flattery as far back as 1887. 'So I have to thank you', writes Wilde on 17th October to him, 'for the charming little printed edition of your poems . . . It shall stand on my shelves, and be a delight to me. You ask me for a manuscript. Yes, I will give you one certainly, but which one would you like . . . Let me see you soon—letters are not enough.'[1] The poems referred to were Le Gallienne's first book *My Ladies' Sonnets* privately printed in Liverpool from funds raised by his office friends there.

As well as charm, he possessed good looks. 'Like Botticelli's Head of Lorenzo' was how William Rothenstein described his appearance. He met his first wife while in Liverpool, a pretty waitress called Mildred Lee. They were married in 1891 and were ideally happy together until her death in childbirth in 1894. His second marriage in 1896 to Julie Norregaard, a well-connected journalist, did not prove a success. They separated in 1898, and he left England for good to live in America where he married his third wife, Irma Stuart-Hinton.

Eva Le Gallienne, daughter by his second wife, has left an interesting brief portrait of her father in her second autobiography *With a Quiet Heart* (1963). She relates how friends had told her mother that 'Richard Le Gallienne was not the sort of man one married'. He was inhabited by two distinct selves or spirits—'the Bishop and the Daymon'. 'These two creatures lived in the soul of one man and fought incessantly for dominion over him. Sometimes the Bishop won the battle, but then the Daymon rose up again and reigned triumphant for a while; the struggle was unending . . . When the Bishop was victorious, no one could have been gentler, wiser, more loving-kind—a quiet scholar, a patient worker, an understanding friend. But all this disappeared when the Daymon got the upper hand; then Richard would be transformed into a mercurial being, violently alive, brilliant, cruel, fascinating and dangerous. The girls, of course, were dazzled by the Daymon, and

[1] *The Letters of Oscar Wilde*

the poor Bishop had a hard time struggling to survive.' She recalls how her father used ruefully to say of his single best-seller *The Quest of the Golden Girl* (1896), 'the publishers got all the gold, and poor Richard got the girls'.

Like his publisher, John Lane, he knew how to exploit a fashion. He tells us in *The Romantic '90's* how, inspired by Pater's rare achievement in prose 'many young pundits declared it the greater art of the two'. Ever adept at staying on the band-wagon, Le Gallienne produced two volumes of *Prose Fancies* (1895 and 1896), the second series of which contained a piece entitled 'The Boom in Yellow'. 'There will always be wearers of the green carnation,' he stated, 'but the popular vogue which green has enjoyed for the last ten or fifteen years is probably passing.' 'Let us dream of this,' he continued, inserting in his 'prose fancy' a trite but clever prose poem, 'a maid with yellow hair, clad in a yellow gown, seated in a yellow room, at the window a yellow sunset, in the grate a yellow fire, at her side a yellow lamplight, on her knees a yellow book.' It reads like a Beardsley cover transcribed, and certainly succeeds in terms of a gimmick.

Part of Le Gallienne's journalistic flair was his gift for having a foot in both worlds—that of the aesthetic *avant-garde* and that of newspaper readership. In 1891, he had joined the Rhymers Club, describing its anthology of 1892 as 'the first concerted attack of the "Bodley Head Poets" on the British Public'.[1] At the same time he had shown himself a Mr Facing-both-Ways when it came to assessing certain ideas found in the work of its co-members. He had, for example, made mock of the excessive adulation of all things Gallic held as a principle by some of the Rhymers. Reviewing Arthur Symons' *Silhouettes*, he neatly deals with this pretention:

> 'Paris, May, 1892.' Thus Mr. Symons dates dedication to a lady of his acquaintance. That mere

[1] *The Romantic '90's*

> superscription means much. Viewed symbolically there is in it a world of pathos. There is always pathos when any one yearns towards a particular class or life, or centre, as it seems, of 'tone', with a feeling that there is the ideal state, to be outside of which is to be 'provincial', *borné*, and other dreadful things. It is the dairymaids' superstition of the 'gentleman', the parvenu's of the 'upper ten', the outcasts of 'society' . . . Had Mr. Symons lived earlier he would doubtless have dated his preface from Alexandria.[1]

Decadence—another shibboleth of the time—came in for some severe treatment when he reviewed the book of verse *Silverpoints* (1893) by John Gray, also a Rhymer:

> Mr. Gray's poems are not so decadent as he would have us suppose. They are luxurious to the last degree, they are subtly cadenced as the song the sirens sang, they will dwell over-unctuously on many forbidden themes—'many whisper things I dare not tell'—they are each separately dedicated to every more or less decadent poet of Mr. Gray's acquaintance . . . But in spite of his neo-Catholicism and his hot-pot erotics, Mr. Gray cannot accomplish that gloating abstraction from the larger life of humanity which marks the decadent.[2]

At the same time, Le Gallienne was careful to balance his censure with praise. 'Criticism', he wrote, 'is the Art of Praise . . . Praise is more important than judgment. It is only at agricultural [sic] societies that men dare sit in judgment upon the rose.'[3]

In a similar way, his own verse reveals an ambivalent attitude to *fin-de-siècle* aestheticism. The lines 'To the Reader' in his *English Poems* (1892) oppose to these new 'strange green flowers' out of France 'English daisies',

[1] *Retrospective Reviews* (1896)
[2] Ibid.
[3] Ibid.

'English larks', and 'English love'. *The Decadent to his Soul*—a rather over-written piece—is a not uningenious verse-critique of the Huysman cult of perversity found in *À Rebours* (1884), the bible of many *fin-de-siècle* writers. None of this prevented him, however, from parading his own eroticism, as in the poem *Neaera's Hair*:[1]

> O thy body, sweet sweet body,
>   let me drink and drink and drink!
> Canst thou let me, like the minstrel,
>   die upon the fountain's brink?
> Love, O Love, what *art* Thou? tell me:
>   is this heaven, hell or where?
> All I know is that I kiss thee,
>   lying in thy yellow hair.

In his attitude, both to the poet and the reader, he knew how to have his cake and eat it too.

Few of Le Gallienne's own poems are unflawed. Trite or mawkish lines succeed others sustained by a proper lyrical impulse. His poem *Song* which originally appeared in *The Yellow Book*, inspired by the memory of his first wife, shows his failure to maintain a poetical level:

> She's somewhere in the sunlight strong
> Her tears are in the falling rain,
> She calls me in the wind's soft song.
> And with the flowers she comes again;
>
> Yon bird is but her messenger,
> The moon is but her silver car,
> Yea! sun and moon are sent by her
> And every wistful, waiting star.

The genuine sense of a numinous presence conveyed in the first quatrain degenerates in the second into poeticism and over-strained statement.

The classical assessment of Le Gallienne's poetry is that

[1] *English Poems*

which Lionel Johnson made in a letter to his friend Katherine Tynan:[1]

> *Prettiness;* not beauty, which implies more imaginative thought and faith, than he possesses. Sensitive by temperament, and feels the *sentiment* of beautiful things in art and life, not their *truth.* A persistent note of—not vulgarity, nor bad taste—but of unconscious familiarity in a bad sense. He belittles things by his touch. When his subject is in itself trivial he can be charming: when it is high he does not rise to it. He prattles, chatters, which he thinks natural and simple: in dread of the 'academic' he becomes impertinent. A real love of poetry, utterly undisciplined and unintelligent: he is never to be trusted. Has enough culture not to be a 'self-taught' genius: and not enough to desire the discipline, the labour, the pains of art. Now and then is happily inspired, and is never quite contemptible: but usually very irritating. Conceivable, that he might write an Endymion: impossible that he should ever write Hyperion or the Odes. Is too much the 'professional' poet, thinking of Chatterton and Keats and Shelley. Should take a long course of Arnold and Dr. Johnson. Contrives to get a certain curious *personality* into his work, which either fascinates or exasperates.

'Is too much the professional poet.' With his green velveteen jacket and massive mop of luxurious curly hair (which Max Beerbohm mocked in his caricature of him, giving him *two* top-hats, one on either side of the parting), Le Gallienne certainly looked the part. To apply what he said of William Sharp to himself, 'If only he had been as good a poet as he was good-looking!'

All this is undoubtedly true; but one can too easily

[1] *Literary Essays of Ezra Pound,* ed. with an Introduction by T. S. Eliot

underestimate him. Symons has been called 'the journalist of the movement',[1] but was tempermentally unsuited to be that—too proudly fastidious, self-conscious, and aloof. ('The newspaper is the plague . . . of the modern world . . . The public has never known good art from bad.'[2]) It was Le Gallienne, in fact, who acted as an important go-between, linking journalism with literature. His prose is always readable; and if most of his verse proves expendable matter, it was necessary to him in order to give a sense of solidarity with those who *were* poets and a feeling of sympathy for their work. Le Gallienne was a generous critic, though the range of his mind was limited. The manifesto which he printed to his *Retrospective Reviews*, 'Some first and second Principles of Criticism' are amusing, good-tempered and liberal in their statement: 'A necessary gift for the critic of poetry is—the love of it'; 'the greatest critic is he who can appreciate the greatest number of beautiful things'; 'a gentleman is always a gentleman—even when he writes anonymous criticism'.

Le Gallienne died on 15th September 1947 at Mentone where he had been living for a number of years.

A Ballad of London

Ah, London! London! our delight,
Great flower that opens but at night,
Great City of the midnight sun,
Whose day begins when day is done.

Lamp after lamp against the sky
Opens a sudden beaming eye,
Leaping alight on either hand,
The iron lilies of the Strand.

[1] *Memoirs of a Victorian* by Edgar Jepson (1933)
[2] 'Fact in Literature' (*Studies in Prose and Verse*) (1904)

Like dragonflies, the hansoms hover,
With jewelled eyes, to catch the lover,
The streets are full of lights and loves,
Soft gowns, and flutter of soiled doves.

Upon thy petals butterflies,
But at thy root, some say, there lies
A world of weeping trodden things,
Poor worms that have not eyes or wings.

From out corruption of their woe
Springs this bright flower that charms us so,
Men die and rot deep out of sight
To keep this jungle-flower bright.

Paris and London, World-Flowers twain
Wherewith the World-Tree blooms again,
Since Time hath gathered Babylon.
And withered Rome still withers on.

Sidon and Tyre were such as ye,
How bright they shone upon the tree!
But Time had gathered, both are gone,
And no man sails to Babylon.

Ah, London! London! our delight,
For thee, too, the eternal night,
And Circe Paris hath no charm
To stay Time's unrelenting arm.

RICHARD LE GALLIENNE

To My Wife, Mildred

Dear wife, there is no word in all my songs
But unto thee belongs:
Though I indeed before our true day came
Mistook thy star in many a wandering flame,
Singing to thee in many a fair disguise,
Calling to thee in many another's name,
Before I knew thine everlasting eyes.

Faces that fled me like a haunted fawn
I followed singing, deeming it was Thou,
Seeking this face that on our pillow now
Glimmers behind thy golden hair like dawn,
And, like a setting moon, within my breast
Sinks down each night to rest.

Moon follows moon before the great moon flowers,
Moon of the wild wild honey that is ours;
Long must the tree strive up in leaf and root,
Before it bear the golden-hearted fruit:
And shall great Love at once perfected spring,
Nor grow by steps like any other thing?

The lawless love that would not be denied,
The love that waited, and in waiting died,
The love that met and mated, satisfied.

Ah, love, 'twas good to climb forbidden walls,
Who would not follow where his Juliet calls?
'Twas good to try and love the angel's way,
With starry souls untainted of the clay;
But, best the love where earth and heaven meet,
The god made flesh and dwelling in us, sweet.

Beauty Accurst

I am so fair that wheresoe'er I wend
  Men yearn with strange desire to kiss my face,
Stretch out their hands to touch me as I pass,
  And women follow me from place to place.

A poet writing honey of his dear
  Leaves the wet page—ah! leaves it long to dry.
The bride forgets it is her marriage-morn,
  The bridegroom too forgets as I go by.

Within the street where my strange feet shall stray
  All markets hush and traffickers forget,
In my gold head forget their meaner gold,
  The poor man grows unmindful of his debt.

Two lovers kissing in a secret place,
  Should I draw nigh—will never kiss again;
I come between the king and his desire,
  And where I am all loving else is vain.

Lo! when I walk along the woodland way
  Strange creatures leer at me with uncouth love
And from the grass reach upward to my breast,
  And to my mouth lean from the boughs above.

The sleepy kine move round me in desire
  And press their oozy lips upon my hair,
Toads kiss my feet and creatures of the mire,
  The snails will leave their shells to watch me there.

But all this worship, what is it to me?
  I smite the ox and crush the toad in death:
I only know I am so very fair,
  And that the world was made to give me breath.

I only wait the hour when God shall rise
  Up from the star where he so long hath sat,
And bow before the wonder of my eyes
  And set *me* there—I am so fair as that.

To the Reader

Art was a palace once, things great and fair,
And strong and holy, found a temple there:
Now 'tis a lazar-house of leprous men.
O shall we hear an English song again!
Still English larks mount in the merry morn,
An English May still brings an English thorn,
Still English daisies up and down the grass,
Still English love for English lad and lass—
Yet youngsters blush to sing an English song!

Thou nightingale that for six hundred years
Sang to the world—O art thou husht at last!
For, not of thee this new voice in our ears,
Music of France that once was of the spheres;
And not of thee these strange green flowers that spring
From daisy roots and seem to bear a sting.

Thou Helicon of numbers 'undefiled',
Forgive that 'neath the shadow of thy name,
England, I bring a song of little fame;
Not as one worthy but as loving thee,
Not as a singer, only as a child.

Lord Alfred Douglas

1870-1945

LORD ALFRED DOUGLAS, third son of John Sholto Douglas—the 'screaming scarlet Marquess' as Wilde called him—was born at Ham Hill near Worcester, on 22nd October 1870.

The life of Lord Alfred (once described as 'the most complete cad in history')[1] has been much publicised. He himself has given us his (sometimes contrary) accounts of his relationship with Wilde: *Oscar Wilde and Myself*, 1914; *Autobiography*, 1929; and *Oscar Wilde: A Summing-up*, 1940. In addition, there exists *The Life of Lord Alfred Douglas* by William Freeman, 1948, and Rupert Croft-Cook's *Bosie*.

Lord Alfred's relationship with Wilde was the centremost affair of his life. As Hesketh Pearson remarks, 'Far from being wrecked by his friendship with Wilde, his reputation was made by it. He became a figure of note, about whom people talked or whispered. Most of his books found a wide circle of readers, not because he himself was interesting but because of the general interest in Wilde.'[2] This is written by an Oscar partisan but must be taken as substantially the case. The memorable meeting of Wilde

[1] Sir Herbert Read: *The Listener* (8th December 1949)
[2] *The Life of Oscar Wilde* (1954)

and Lord Alfred has been related by the letter in *A Summing-up*:

> I met Wilde for the first time in 1891 when Lionel Johnson, the Wykehamist poet, who had been with me at Oxford and for whom I had a great friendship, took me to see him in his house, 16 Tite Street, Chelsea. I was then twenty years [and Wilde thirty-six]. Oscar took a violent fancy to me at sight . . . I was from the first flattered that a man so distinguished as he was should pay me so much attention and attach so much importance . . . to all my views and preferences and whims.

Campbell Dodgson, engaged as a tutor to Lord Alfred, wrote to his friend Lionel Johnson: 'Bosie is beautiful and fascinating, but quite wicked.'[1]

It was the beauty which Wilde noticed first. 'He is quite like a narcissus,' he wrote of his 'honey-haired' protégé, 'so white and gold . . . I worship him.'[2] And then to Lord Alfred himself: 'You are the atmosphere of beauty through which I see life; you are the incarnation of all lovely things.'[3]

It was when the long ruinous honeymoon was over that Wilde found wickedness uppermost. Less than six months before his death he was declaring to his friend Robert Ross: 'Bosie I have not seen for a week. I feel sure he will do nothing. Boys, brandy, and betting monopolise his soul.'[4]

'. . . Do nothing'—no, Wilde was wrong about this; since Lord Alfred left behind him no inconsiderable body of work. At Oxford he had edited the later notorious undergraduate periodical *The Spirit Lamp* from November 1892 to June 1893. Two of his works belong, in fact, to the years in which Wilde knew him. His first book *Poems* (1896) was published in Paris, with prose versions in

[1] 8th February 1893 (*The Letters of Oscar Wilde*)
[2] To Robert Ross (May–June 1892). (Ibid.)
[3] August 1894. (Ibid.)
[4] *Circa* 29th June 1900. (Ibid.)

French on the opposite page to the English original, by Eugéne Tardieu, translator of Wilde's novel *The Picture of Dorian Gray*. This contained the poem *Two Loves* with the concluding tell-tale line

> I am the Love that dare not speak its name.

The piece had appeared in *Chameleon*, an Oxford undergraduate magazine; and was later quoted in Court. After its appearance in *Poems*, Lord Alfred did not reprint it until it appeared, with an apologia, in his *Lyrics* (1935).

His next publication was *The City of the Soul* (1899). It was published anonymously by Grant Richards, and was reviewed glowingly in the *Outlook* (3rd June) by Lionel Johnson, whose notice bore the caption *A Great Unknown* and opened with the welcoming words 'Among crowds of clever versifiers here comes a poet.' Wilde, writing to the publisher Leonard Smithers, give this picture of the poet in his hour of triumph. 'Bosie had vine leaves in his hair and saw the moon at mid-day . . . [He] is naturally in high spirits over his first review in the *Outlook;* it certainly is splendid.'[1]

In 1902 he had made a run-away marriage with the heiress and poet Olive Custance. My thoughts like bees explore all sweetest things',[2] he wrote in a sonnet sequence to her in 1907. The marriage did not prove lasting, however, and they lived apart though on friendly terms. In 1909, Lord Alfred published a volume entitled *Sonnets.* This was followed by *Collected Poems* in 1919, *Complete Poems* in 1928, and *Collected Satires* in 1926. In 1935 there was issued a fuller book of *Sonnets* along with a uniform volume of *Lyrics*.

In addition to this there appeared *The True History of Shakespeare's Sonnets* (1933)—a re-reading of Shakespeare's sequence based on Wilde's story *The Portrait of Mr. W. H.* which appeared first in *Blackwood's Edinburgh Magazine* in July 1889. The interesting (and to Lord

[1] 8th June 1899 (*The Letters of Oscar Wilde*)
[2] 'To Olive' (*Complete Poems*) (1926)

Alfred, the conclusive) element in his book was the evidence produced by him, after research in the archives of Canterbury Cathedral, that a 'Master Will Hewes formerly apprenticed to John Marlowe [father of the dramatist]' was a substantial person. In 1943, two years before his death, Lord Alfred delivered to the Royal Society of Literature an embattled 'traditionalist' address on *The Principles of Poetry* in which he spoke of T.S. Eliot as 'the supreme example of the contempt of form'. Lively, lyrical, or irrascible, this hardly confirms Wilde's prophesy in 1899 that he would 'do nothing'.

Before that date Wilde had indeed been Lord Alfred's chief enthusiast. Writing to the poet in August 1894 he praised 'that light lyrical grace which you always have', and told Leonard Smithers: 'He is a most delicate and exquisite poet . . . far the finest of all the young poets in England. You have got to publish his next volume; it is full of lovely lyrics, flute-music and moon-music, and sonnets in ivory and gold.'[1]

Making all due allowance for Wilde's epistolary performance in the role of 'The Critic as Artist', the appreciation is not without substance. Herbert Palmer, in his *Post-Victorian Poetry*, describes him as 'a sonnet-writer of outstanding distinction' and as the author of 'at least one narrative poem of high excellence'.

Part, at least, of Lord Alfred's epitaph might be found in one of his sonnets to his wife:

> I have been profligate of happiness
> And reckless of the world's hostility,
> The blessed part has not been given to me
> Gladly to suffer fools.

In 1911 he was received into the Roman Catholic Church, and from that time forward, we have the spectacle of a man struggling, with the support of his religion, against the family history of egoism, vanity, and violence.

[1] 1st October 1897 (*The Letters of Oscar Wilde*)

Mostly he is observed falling down; but we cannot help but be impressed by the 'final perseverance' which he shows in the long conflict with his own unruly nature.

Lord Alfred died at Monk's Farm, Lancing, on 20th March 1945.

Impression de Nuit

LONDON

See what a mass of gems the city wears
Upon her broad live bosom! row on row
Rubies and emeralds and amethysts glow.
See! that huge circle like a necklace, stares
With thousands of bold eyes to heaven, and dares
The golden stars to dim the lamps below,
And in the mirror of the mire I know
The moon has left her image unawares.

That's the great town at night: I see her breasts,
Pricked out with lamps they stand like huge black
  towers.
I think they move! I hear her panting breath.
And that's her head where the tiara rests.
And in her brain, through lanes as dark as death,
Men creep like thoughts . . . The lamps are like pale
  flowers.

LORD ALFRED DOUGLAS

OSCAR WILDE

Plainte Eternelle

The sun sinks down, the tremulous daylight dies.
  (Down their long shafts the weary sunbeams glide.)
  The white-winged ships drift with the falling tide,
Come back, my love, with pity in your eyes!

The tall white ships drift with the falling tide.
  (Far, far away I hear the semews' cries.)
  Come back, my love, with pity in your eyes!
There is no room now in my heart for pride.

Come back, come back! with pity in your eyes.
  (The night is dark, the sea is fierce and wide.)
  There is no room now in my heart for pride,
Though I become the scorn of all the wise.

I have no place now in my heart for pride.
  (The moon and stars have fallen from the skies.)
  Though I become the scorn of all the wise,
Thrust, if you will, sharp arrows in my side.

Let me become the scorn of all the wise.
  (Out of the East I see the morning rise.)
  Thrust, if you will, sharp arrows in my side,
Play with my tears and feed upon my sighs.

Wound me with swords, put arrows in my side.
  (On the white sea the haze of noon-day lies.)
  Play with my tears and feed upon my sighs,
But come, my love, before my heart has died.

Drink my salt tears and feed upon my sighs.
(Westward the evening goes with one red stride.)
Come back, my love, before my heart has died,
Down sinks the sun, the tremulous daylight dies.

Come back! my love, before my heart has died.
(Out of the South I see the pale moon rise.)
Down sinks the sun, the tremulous daylight dies,
The white-winged ships drift with the falling tide.

The City of the Soul: II

What shall we do, my soul, to please the King?
Seeing he hath no pleasure in the dance,
And hath condemned the honeyed utterance
Of silver flutes and mouths made round to sing.
Along the wall red roses climb and cling,
And oh! my prince, lift up thy countenance,
For there be thoughts like roses that entrance
More than the languors of soft lute-playing.

Think how the hidden things that poets see
In amber eves or mornings crystalline,
Hide in the soul their constant quenchless light,
Till, called by some celestial alchemy,
Out of forgotten depths, they rise and shine
Like buried treasure on Midsummer night.

LORD ALFRED DOUGLAS

Sonnet, dedicated to those French men of letters (Messrs. Zola, Copée, Sardou and others) who refused to compromise their spotless reputations or imperil their literary exclusiveness by signing a merciful petition in favour of Oscar Wilde.

Not all the singers of a thousand years
Can open English prisons. No. Though hell
Opened for Tracian Orpheus, now the spell
Of song and art is powerless as the tears
That love has shed. You that were full of fears,
And mean self-love, shall live to know full well
That you yourselves, not he, were pitiable
When you met mercy's voice with frowns or jeers.

And did you ask who signed the plea with you?
Fools! It was signed already with the sign
Of great dead men, of God-like Socrates,
Shakespeare and Plato and the Florentine
Who conquered form. And all your petty crew
Once, and once only, might have stood with these.

1896

Sonnet on the Sonnet

To see the moment holds a madrigal,
To find some cloistered place, some hermitage
For free devices, some deliberate cage
Wherein to keep wild thoughts like birds in thrall;
To eat sweet honey and to taste black gall,
To fight with form, to wrestle and to rage,
Till at the last upon the conquered page
The shadows of created Beauty fall.

This is the sonnet, this is all delight
Of every flower that blows in every Spring,
And all desire of every desert place;
This is the joy that fills a cloudy night
When bursting from her misty following,
A perfect moon wins to an empty space.

Le Balcon

(FROM THE FRENCH OF BAUDELAIRE)

Mother of Memories! O mistress-queen!
Oh! all my joy and all my duty thou!
The beauty of caresses that have been,
The evenings and the hearth remember now,
Mother of Memories! O mistress-queen!

LORD ALFRED DOUGLAS

The evenings burning with the glowing fire,
And on the balcony, the rose-stained nights!
How sweet, how kind you were, my soul's desire.
We said things wonderful as chrysolites,
When evening burned beside the glowing fire.

How fair the Sun is in the evening!
How strong the soul, how high the heaven's high
  tower!
O first and last of every worshipped thing,
Your odorous heart's-blood filled me like a flower.
How fair the sun is in the evening!

The night grew deep between us like a pall,
And in the dark I guessed your shining eyes,
And drank your breath, O sweet, O honey-gall!
Your little feet slept on me sister-wise.
The night grew deep between us like a pall.

I can call back the days desirable,
And live all bliss again between your knees,
For where else can I find that magic spell
Save in your heart and in your Mysteries?
I can call back the days desirable.

These vows, these scents, these kisses infinite,
Will they like young suns climbing up the skies
Rise up from some unfathomable pit,
Washed in the sea from all impurities?
O vows, O scents, O kisses infinite!

Harmonie du Soir

(FROM THE FRENCH OF BAUDELAIRE)

Now is the hour when, swinging in the breeze,
Each flower, like a censer, sheds its sweet.
The air is full of scents and melodies,
O languorous waltz! O swoon of dancing feet!

Each flower, like a censer, sheds its sweet,
The violins are like sad souls that cry,
O languorous waltz! O swoon of dancing feet!
A shrine of Death and Beauty is the sky.

The violins are like sad souls that cry,
Poor souls that hate the vast black night of Death;
A shrine of Death and Beauty is the sky.
Drowned in red blood, the Sun gives us his breath.

This soul that hates the vast black night of Death
Takes all the luminous past back tenderly,
Drowned in red blood, the Sun gives up his breath.
Thine image like a monstrance shines in me.

Oscar Wilde

1854–1900

OSCAR FINGAL O'FLAHERTIE WILLS WILDE, the younger son of a celebrated Irish surgeon, was born in Dublin on 16th October 1854.

The story of his colourful tragic life has been too often told for it to need recounting again here. How this tragedy felt from the inside may perhaps be realised by reading Wilde's famous 'De Profundis' letter,[1] written from prison to Lord Alfred Douglas, and the latter's *Oscar Wilde: A Summing Up* (1940). How it felt to Wilde, he has graphically expressed. 'I also had my illusions. I thought life was going to be a brilliant comedy, and that you were to be one of many graceful figures in it. I found it to be a revolting and repellent tragedy, and that the sinister occasion of the great catastrophe . . . was yourself, stripped of the mask of joy and pleasure by which you, no less than I, had been deceived and led astray.' It is to this catastrophe that we owe Wilde's one achievement as a major poet—*The Ballad of Reading Gaol*—though critics differ widely on the stature they accord it.

Lord Alfred Douglas, in whose villa at Posilippo the poem was completed, was constant in his enthusiasm for it. 'From the formal point of view,' he tells us, 'it was modelled on Coleridge's *Ancient Mariner*, and it may also be said to have owed something to Thomas Hood's

[1] *The Letters of Oscar Wilde*

Eugene Aram. Both Hood and Wilde dealt with a real murderer in real life, but Wilde's poem is infinitely superior to Hood's, and . . . easily holds its own with Coleridge's.'[1] For Henley, on the other hand, 'the trail of the minor poet is over it all'.

The most penetrating case against the poem has probably been stated by Arthur Symons who, however, was not without *partis pris*. Wilde had met Symons in 1890 when Wilde was editor of *Woman's World* to which Symons had contributed a poem and an article on Villiers de l'Isle Adam. Wilde began as a declared admirer of his work,[2] but his later attitude was one of joking contempt. 'An egoist without an ego' was perhaps his unkindest shaft. Symons presumably heard of this, and though he reviewed *The Ballad of Reading Gaol* much to Wilde's satisfaction ('admirably written, and most . . . artistic in its mode of approval') in 1898, he bided his time till Wilde's death in November 1900. In the next year he wrote his article *An Artist in Attitudes: Oscar Wilde*,[3] the first part of which is concerned with Wilde's by then famous last poem.

'When *The Ballad of Reading Gaol* was first published,' wrote Symons, 'it seemed to some people that such a return to . . . real things was precisely what was most required to bring into relation, both with life and art, an extraordinary talent, so little in relation to matters of common experience. In this poem, where a style formed on other lines seems startled at finding itself used for such new purposes, we see a great spectacular intellect, to which, at last, pity and terror have come in their own person, and no longer as puppets in a play . . . And now, having become so newly acquainted with what is pitiful, and what seems most unjust, in the arrangement of human affairs, it has gone . . . to an extreme, on the one hand, humanitarianism, on the other, realism, at more than their just valuation, in matters of art.'

[1] *Oscar Wilde: The Summing-up*
[2] Wilde to Leonard Smithers, 15th March 1898: *The Letters of Oscar Wilde*
[3] *Studies in Prose and Verse*

But it was when he started to generalise that Symons' criticism proved most destructive. Wilde's 'intellect', he asserted, 'was dramatic, and the whole man was not so much a personality as an attitude. Without being a sage, he maintained the attitude of a sage; without being a poet, he maintained the attitude of a poet; without being an artist, he maintained the attitude of an artist . . . Of the purely poetical quality he had almost nothing.'

This is both correct and incorrect; correct as to the bulk of Wilde's poetry, but incorrect as to that small portion of it where genuine realisation takes place. It is true that the 'attitude of a poet' which Wilde so readily assumed provided him with a ready-made rhetoric, a sort of imagination-saving device. There is a blatancy of tone, a stridency of sense impression, which is both intense and yet unreal, in this consistent pose of language:

> Priest-like, he wore a robe more white than foam,
>   And, king-like, swathed himself in royal red,
>   Three crowns of gold rose up upon his head:
> In splendour and in light the Pope passed home.[1]

The glow which this rhetoric cast upon things approximated more to the luminous tints of gorgeous technicolour than the light of common day. For the latter the reader must turn to *The Ballad of Reading Gaol*, where even there its presence is intermittent. There is rhetoric of a somewhat brazen order in the first two lines of the following stanza, the last four lines of which, however, express a vivacious sensibility:

> The warders strutted up and down,
>   And kept their herd of brutes,
> Their uniforms were spic and span,
>   And they wore their Sunday suits,
> But we knew the work they had been at,
>   By the quick-lime on their boots.

It seems that the unevenness of the *Ballad* was apparent

[1] 'Easter Day' (*Poems*) (1881)

even to Wilde himself. 'I think bits of the poem very good now,' he wrote to Leonard Smithers (Friday, 1st October 1897), 'but I will never again out-Kipling Henley.'[1]

During the 'nineties, Wilde published only two new volumes of verse; the *Ballad* and *The Sphinx* which appeared in 1894. This highly artificial *tour de force* is little to the taste of today. Its rhetoric is a Romantic one—the near-Eastern eloquence of Flaubert's *La Tentation de Saint Antoine* translated into verse. One of the few defences of this poem has been made by Herbert Palmer in his *Post-Victorian Poetry* (1938):

> Oscar Wilde's poetry is chiefly flowery pastiche. But in *The Sphinx* he generally transmutes his derivations very cunningly. It is not merely that he took Tennyson's *In Memoriam* stanza and wrote it out as two lines instead of four, but he has very operatively proved that Tennyson's rhymes are much more effective as internal and cross rhymes than as end rhymes, sign-pointing, too, to a more flexible stanza and greater speed and resonance in the metrical beat. Though the rhyme arrangement and metrical form have been borrowed from Tennyson, and the theme suggested by Poe's *Raven*, the outstanding literary background is deftly fused Baudelaire and Swinburne, while the *Rubayat* of Omar Khayyam has helped to create his Eastern atmosphere.
>
> Come forth, my lovely seneschal! So
> somnolent, so statuesque!
> Come forth you exquisite grotesque!
> half-woman and half-animal.

Wilde himself thought most highly of his poem. Although it did not appear until 1894, he had worked on it from his Oxford days till 1883 or thereabouts. 'Also', he wrote to John Lane on signing a publisher's agreement, 'the selection of reviews to which the book is sent must be

[1] *The Letters of Oscar Wilde*

a matter of arrangement between you and your partner and me. A book of this kind—very rare and curious—must not be thrown into the gutter of English journalism.'[1] His own words are perhaps the best appreciation of Wilde's poetry.

After winning the Newdigate Prize at Oxford with his composition *Ravenna* in 1878, he published his first book *Poems* in 1881, a limited edition of which in 1892 had a binding of 'gold smeared in tired purple'.[2] The collected edition of his poems appeared in 1908, containing a section of 'Uncollected Poems' written between 1876 and 1893. Particulars of the original publication of each poem will be found in *A Bibliography of the Poems of Oscar Wilde* by Stuart Mason, 1907.

Oscar Wilde died in Paris on 30th November 1900, a convert to Roman Catholicism.

With a Copy of 'A House of Pomegranates'

Go, little book,
To him who, on a lute with horns of pearl,
Sang of the white feet of the Golden Girl:
And bid him look
Into thy pages: it may hap that he
May find that golden maiden dance through thee.

1893

[1] Ibid.

[2] O.W. to Grant Richards (*The Letters of Oscar Wilde*)

The reference is to Richard Le Gallienne, who had published a romance *The Quest of The Golden Girl*

FROM

The Ballad of Reading Gaol

IN MEMORIAM
C.T.W.
SOMETIME TROOPER OF THE ROYAL HORSE GUARDS, OBIT H.M. PRISON, READING, BERKSHIRE, JULY 7, 1896

I

He did not wear his scarlet cloak,
For blood and wine are red,
And blood and wine were on his hands
When they found him with the dead,
The poor dead woman whom he loved,
And murdered in her bed.

He walked among the Trial Men
In a suit of shabby grey;
A cricket cap was on his head,
And his step seemed light and gay;
But I never saw a man who looked
So wistfully at the day.

I never saw a man who looked
With such a wistful eye
Upon that little tent of blue
Which prisoners call the sky,
And at every drifting cloud that went
With sails of silver by.

I walked, with other souls in pain,
  Within another ring,
And was wondering if the man had done
  A great or little thing,
When a voice behind me whispered low,
  'That fellow's got to swing.'

Dear Christ! the very prison walls
  Suddenly seemed to reel
And the sky above my head became
  Like a casque of scorching steel;
And, though I was a soul in pain,
  My pain I could not feel.

I only knew what hunted thought
  Quickened his step, and why
He looked upon the garish day
  With such a wistful eye;
The man had killed the thing he loved,
  And so he had to die.

Yet each man kills the thing he loves,
  By each let this be heard,
Some do it with a bitter look,
  Some with a flattering word,
The coward does it with a kiss,
  The brave man with a sword!

Some kill their love when they are young,
  And some when they are old;
Some strangle with the hands of Lust,
  Some with the hands of Gold:
The kindest use a knife, because
  The dead so soon grow cold.

Some love too little, some too long,
  Some sell, and others buy;
Some do the deed with many tears,
  And some without a sight:
For each man kills the thing he loves,
  Yet each man does not die.

He does not die a death of shame
  On a day of dark disgrace,
Nor have a noose about his neck,
  Nor a cloth about his face,
Nor drop feet foremost through the floor
  Into an empty space.

. . . .

He does not sit with silent men
  Who watch him night and day;
Who watch him when he tries to weep,
  And when he tries to pray;
Who watch him lest himself should rob
  The prison of its prey.

He does not wake at dawn to see
  Dread figures throng his room,
The shivering Chaplain robed in white,
  The Sheriff stern with gloom,
And the Governor all in shiny black,
  With the yellow face of Doom.

He does not rise in piteous haste
  To put on convict clothes,
While some coarse-mouthed Doctor gloats,
    and notes
  Each new and nerve-twitched pose,
Fingering a watch whose little ticks
  Are like horrible hammer-blows.

He does not know that sickening thirst
  That sands one's throat, before
The hangman with his gardener's gloves
  Slips through the padded door,
And binds one with three leathern thongs,
  That the throat may thirst no more.

He does not bend his head to hear
  The Burial Service read,
Nor, while the terror of his soul
  Tells him he is not dead,
Cross his own coffin, as he moves
  Into that hideous shed.

He does not stare upon the air
  Through a little roof of glass:
He does not pray with lips of clay
  For his agony to pass;
Nor feel upon his shuddering cheek
  The kiss of Caiaphas.

HENRY JAMES
Selected Tales 18*s*

STORM JAMESON
Morley Roberts 10*s* 6*d*

EDGAR JEPSON
Memories of an Edwardian 10*s* 6*d*

LIONEL JOHNSON
The Complete Poems, Introduction by Iain Fletcher 26*s*

RICHARD LE GALLIENNE
From a Paris Garret 21*s*

ROGER LHOMBREAUD
Arthur Symons—a Critical Biography 42*s*

EDWARD FITZGERALD
The Rubaiyat of Omar Khayyam 5*s*

GRANT RICHARDS
Author Hunting, Introduction by Alex Waugh 25*s*

ARTHUR SYMONS
Aubrey Beardsley 10*s*

R. WHITTINGTON-EGAN and
GEOFFREY SMERDON
The Quest of the Golden Boy—the Life and Letters of Richard Le Gallienne 50*s*

OSCAR WILDE
Four Plays 12*s*
Intentions 8*s* 6*d*
A House of Pomegranates 8*s* 6*d*
Lord Arthur Savile's Crime 8*s* 6*d*
Salomé 4*s* 6*d*
The Ballad of Reading Gaol 5*s*